The Future of Healthcare Software Business in Canada

George O. Obikoya

Table of Content

Executive Summary

The increasing appreciation of the potential benefits of software in the achievement of the dual healthcare delivery objectives of qualitative health services provision while simultaneously reducing health spending is creating immense business opportunities for software firms but also revealing potential challenges. The ability of these firms to harness their competencies in ascertaining these opportunities, evident and cryptic, and in overcoming market obstacles would determine their odds to survive let alone, thrive. With healthcare delivery becoming more patient-centered, the expectations of service delivery by the consumer more sophisticated and complex, healthcare jurisdictions under increasing budgetary pressure as health pending soars relentlessly, the transformational challenges healthcare organizations face unabated, and the debate over the need or otherwise for a parallel private health system persisting, Canada's health sector, is indeed, evolving. The outcome of this process would be the product of the interplay of a variety of issues, whose underlying processes healthcare software firms need to explore to determine and actualize their strategic value propositions and market orientation. That these issues cut across domains, health and non-health, underscores the complexity of the healthcare delivery process on the one hand, and on the other, the extent of the potential markets for innovative software products and services, particularly in a sector with a legendary lag in healthcare ICT adoption, relative to similarly information-intensive industries.

The need for the health sector to reinvent itself is inherent in the perpetual flux manifest in these issues, from that of the need for preparedness for and response to the potential cataclysm of an emergent virus to that for inventive integrated customer relationship management or sector-wide supply chain solutions, for examples. It is therefore equally imperative that the health sector meets the challenges that confront it at every phase of its evolution to progress in its continuing transition along the quality progress spectrum, which makes its investments in the technologies that could both enable and accentuate this progress inevitable. The market opportunities that this would present to healthcare software firms would not be exclusively vertical. In fact, the increased deployment of healthcare software and other ICT within the health system would result in an interlocking cascade that binds both vertical and horizontal markets, creating significant prospects for Canadian software firms, even if some they would need to ferret. These issues and others that drive contemporary healthcare and their bearing on the future of healthcare software and ICT business in Canada we will explore in detail in this e-book. That their influence on the healthcare software industry we cannot discountenance considering the health and economy dyadic, and the potential contributions of this industry on the latter too, further highlights the seriousness with which Canadian software firms need to view these issues, which in our analyses in this e-book, we would attempt to foster.

Introduction

Besides being a critical component of Canada's economic development, the

healthcare software industry is crucial to the future of the country's health sector
in both facilitating the delivery of qualitative health services and in doing so
simultaneously curtailing health spending, which latter has been consuming
increasing portions of the country's gross domestic product (GDP), clearly, an
unsustainable situation left unchecked. The health sector is increasingly aware of
the potential of healthcare information and communication technologies in
helping to achieve these dual healthcare delivery objectives, hence investing
more in them. This is creating immense business opportunities for healthcare
software firms that they might not be exploiting maximally as to do so requires
for example, a comprehensive process cycle analysis of the markets of interest, a
continuous decomposition/exposition process that would reveal the issues and
processes involved with healthcare delivery, and indicate the technology needs
for addressing them.

To be sure, the issues germane to contemporary and future healthcare

delivery in Canada are legion. Some of these issues are health and others non-
health-related. They all would likely involve other sub-issues, and underlying
processes, which play varying roles in determining the outcome of the interplay
of the larger issues and processes, thus, all effectively drivers of the outcome to a
more or less extent. The discovery of the specific roles that these issues and

processes play in healthcare delivery, and the mechanics involved in doing so, are some of the key tasks in which Canadian healthcare software firms would need to engage to appreciate in full, the needs of the health sector markets, both vertical and horizontal, hence to respond to them appropriately. Indeed, these tasks, for example, process cycle analyses, could reveal even some otherwise cryptic business opportunities, and perhaps transform erstwhile challenges into others.

In the mix of opportunities and challenges that the health sector presents the

software industry would emerge the transformational needs of both industries, representing opportunities to actualize their respective objectives, including for example for the former, the achievement of the dual healthcare delivery goals, for the latter, profitability, and for both, positive contributions to the country's sustainable economic development. For these reasons, among others, the onus is not just on the health industry to keep offering the opportunities to Canadian software firms to develop innovative products and services, but also on the latter to respond accordingly, including offering novel value propositions to help both industries realize their objectives, to which the health sector needs also respond equally suitably. We would explore these various issues in this e-book, with emphasis on the dynamic interplay of factors between these two pivotal Canadian industries, and its outcome for both, among many others.

Developments in Healthcare Software Business in Canada

The expansion by 1.2% in the first quarter of 2006 in Canada's ICT sector output (GDP) is remarkable, relative to the 0.8% growth by the Canadian economy overall[1]. Indeed, the growth in Canada's ICT sector has been ongoing, since the last quarter of 2001, having grown by 99% since the first quarter of 1997, about thrice the national economy's growth rate of 37% during the same period as figure 1 shows. The sector's output in the first 2006 quarter was 19% more than at the end of 2001, the entire country's economy growing by 14% during the same period. There is no doubt that the country's ICT industry has being doing well, but could we say the same about its sub-sectors, in particular the software sub-sector, more so in the health sector? ICT manufacturing GDP increased by 1.9% in the first quarter of 2006, that of manufacturing unwavering. There was a fall in ICT output in the first quarter of 2004 in this sub-sector, but it has since been increasing, an increase experts predict would be enduring, growth in real output since 1997, 61%, relative to the country's manufacturing sub-sector's overall of 34% since 1997, and since the end 2001, growth in the sub-sector, 43%[1].

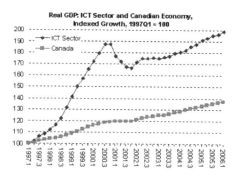

Figure 1: Source: strategis.ic.gc.ca[1]

In order to appreciate fully, the contribution of the software sub-sector to the growth that the ICT sector in Canada has had over the past couple of years, the evolution of software business in the country and in particular, in the health sector, and its likely future directions in the latter, we need to examine these figures a little closer. Compared to the growth in the ICT manufacturing sub-sector, growth in the services sub-sector, 1% in the first quarter of 2006, which incidentally echoes akin growth in overall Canadian services GDP, is smaller, although output in both, overall grew by 14% from the last quarter of 2001 to the first of 2006 as figure 2 shows. ICT sector-services industries have also been growing since the first quarter of 1997, a 112% output growth between the first quarter of 1997 and 2006, significantly better performance than the 39% growth overall in Canadian services, during the same period. Could an improvement in the performance of ICT services not help improve the performance of the Canadian services sector, a major component of the economy, hence that of the country's economy overall? What role could a re-conceptualization of the role of software, and indeed, of healthcare ICT in general, as being much more than an

8

enabler, but indeed, a constitutive, organic element of the intricate processes that underlie the crucial issues involved in actualizing healthcare delivery programs, activities, and events play in this regard? Would this paradigm shift not make a difference to the attitude to, knowledge of, and the practice of software applications in healthcare delivery? If indeed, it did, then we would see dramatic changes in the dynamics of the drivers of the healthcare industry on the one hand, and in the software and healthcare ICT markets on the other, changes that would likely have a domino effect on the country's service sector and the economy at large.

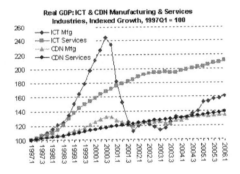

Figure 2: Source: strategis.ic.gc.ca[1]

First quarter ICT manufacturing sub-sector growth was in the main, due to 7.6% growth in the production of communications equipments, that of instruments accounting for 5.1%. Significantly, in the first quarter of 2006, computer and peripheral equipment manufacturing output fell by 6.7%. Would this have likely negative implications for software production, considering the link between software and computers, and if so, how might this effect resonate in the health sector? On the other hand, could the health sector reverse this potential negative impact? Does this mean that the software industry might not have been paying attention to a sector of the economy with the potential to boost its contribution to the country's economic growth and sustainable development? Could even the telecommunications businesses have been missing a potential market segment for which they have or could have developed marketable healthcare products and services collaborating with the software industry? These are pertinent questions the answers to which could reorient the healthcare software and in fact, the entire healthcare ICT industry in the country, improving its GDP and the industry's competitiveness on the global ICT stage. Telecommunications services' 0.7% growth increase made up the major part of the ICT services growth in the first 2006 quarter, a continuation of the pattern since the first quarter of 1997, GDP 2006 first quarter growth, 86%. Indeed, all ICT service industries grew in the quarter in question except the software industry, which in fact declined by 0.6%, although, medium term, its GDP went up by 20% since the 2003 fourth quarter. That the performance of the software industry in Canada, a country that has some of the best software engineers and developers in the world, could decline is cause for concern. Even with the 2.0% output increase in the 2006 first quarter by the data processing services industry, albeit after losses in four successive quarters, and whose output had in fact been falling since 2002's first quarter, by 9.8% overall this period, the software industry as whole no doubt requires some scrutiny[1]. This is more so as improved performance of the software industry has the potential to create employment opportunities, among other benefits, which itself is an index of sustainable economic development. Furthermore, the intricate link between the economy and health also means that the country would be further enhancing its prospects of even greater and more sustained development by having a healthy, productive, and gainfully employed populace, taking the task of improving its economy seriously. Why would it then not focus on the contributions that its economic sectors and sub-sectors could make to these efforts, and in the case of software, why would it not explore the reasons that industry is lagging behind and in particular in its applications in health services provision as a first step toward actualizing these efforts? Indeed, the lag, some would contend in the latter case, being by as much as a decade behind other information-intensive industries such as the banking industry is alarming. Could the country afford not to explore why the software industry seems to be failing to develop desperately needed products and services for an inherently massive market and potential source of economic growth for the country, the health sector? To be sure, with regards job creation, there was a 1.1% rise in ICT employment compared to the country's overall of 0.4% in the 2006 first quarter. ICT services fared better in the 2006 first quarter than the manufacturing sub-sector, growing by 1.1%, which conforms to a similar growth pattern since the 2002 first quarter, above which it is 6.8%. Indeed, employment levels in ICT manufacturing rose by 0.8% in the first quarter of 2006, although still 3.4% below its 2002-second quarter level, 0.1% for manufacturing in the country as a whole, both falling since then, the latter by as much as 4.7%. Contrariwise, employment in the software industry grew in the second and third quarters of 2005, but fell 1.3% in the next, although overall, increased by 20% since the fourth quarter of 2003. Are we going to see a downward trend in employment in the software industry in Canada, do we have to, and if not, what could we do not to have to? Would we not increase employment rate in the industry by preventing it declining further than it already did in the first quarter of 2006? Could not doing something about the status of the software industry result in a downturn in the current encouraging employment growth in the ICT services sub-sector overall in the first 2006 quarter, which in the main was from the data processing services, telecommunications services and computer systems design industries, 2.5%, 1.4% and 0.8%, respectively?

T herefore, we need to seek what we could and should do about maximizing

the potential of the software industry in healthcare delivery. There are of course many different options, but whatever we do would in general invariably require the concerted efforts of all healthcare stakeholders. There is no doubt that the software industry would be the biggest loser in not taking action on this matter, and recent developments in the industry in the U.S for example, suggest that this fact is beginning to dawn on some including key actors in the industry. One such development is the July 26, 2006 announcement by Microsoft to offer healthcare software, a major departure from its usual strategy of promoting the development of industry-specific products by other firms utilizing its operating system and programming tools[2]. Microsoft's first move in this direction was to purchase clinical health care software that doctors and researchers at Washington Hospital Center, a nonprofit hospital in Washington developed, including employing two of the three doctors that developed the software system and forty members of the software development team. With the prospects by hospitals, healthcare providers, and entire health systems being able to deliver qualitative health services simultaneously cutting health spending increasingly irresistible, and perhaps the most massive global market to offer products and services waiting eagerly for them, it is in fact paradoxical that it is taking so long for the software industry to notice the health sector. However, it seems that all that is about to change. According to Peter Neupert, Microsoft's vice president for health strategy, "This represents a change in our strategy... This is the start for Microsoft. We're just getting started." This is a major shift from the company's approach of supplying other firms with operating systems, database software and programming tools for use in developing applications for specific industries, for example the banking industry. Microsoft is buying the software system, called Azyxxi, designed to obtain and promptly display patient information from a variety of sources such as ECGs, X-Rays, and other radio-diagnostic sources. The software, initially installed and used at the Washington Hospital Center's ER unit in 1996, and which six other hospital have since adopted, Mr. Nuepert noted that Azyxxi is "our foundation...You'll find us expanding to a suite of health care solutions." There are concerns in some quarters that Microsoft, would be plunging headlong into competition with its erstwhile partners venturing in this new direction, that the software is proprietary and untested outside its restricted domain, and that it has no customer base in this market segment as its competitors already do. Nonetheless, Microsoft's entry into this market signals a new era in the healthcare software business that would be beneficial to both the software and health industries. This is more so considering not just the likely positive effect of the heightened competition that would ensue on research and innovation, hence product and service differentiation, but also on price, and on the quality of healthcare delivery overall. This is not to mention the likely increase in job creation, and on the topography of the industry with possible mergers and takeovers, all increasing the vibrancy of the industry with potential positive effects on the overall economy. According to Dr. Craig F. Feied, a principal designer of the software, Azyxxi is mainly a "data exploration engine" that characteristically works with legacy clinical systems facilitating data sharing among disparate systems, but does not replace them. This makes the software invaluable in meeting the crucial need for speedy data and information collection, collation, and display from various sources of comprehensive regional and national health information networks, which the U.S, Canada, and many other countries aspire to build. Azyxxi has an enviable reputation, the ER capacity at the Washington Hospital Center, up from its installation in 1995 from 37,000 patients per annum, to 80,000, and hours of waiting for care slashed considerably, about two thirds of patients seen in the ER diagnosed, treated or admitted if necessary, typically within three hours. Yet, staff compliment increased by a mere 5%, and rooms added, few.

According to Dr Feied, the software solved the problem of patients waiting for care because doctors lacked prompt and real-time access to patient health information at the point of care, noting, "We weren't doctor-poor or bed-poor, we were information-poor". Microsoft plans to replicate and commercialize the benefits of Azyxxi, with no doubt in the process, opening the way for the development of more creative and valuable healthcare software, in particular as it is also conceptualizing software as a service. This is a concept which, applied in the health sector, could revolutionize the sector and bring about the achievement of the dual healthcare delivery objectives mentioned earlier much quicker in those countries that also embrace this concept[3].

Microsoft CEO, Steve Ballmer, noted at the firm's financial analyst meeting on July 27, 2006 that it is fast moving toward developing products fundable by ads and offered via the Internet. According to Ballmer, "Software is becoming a service...Embracing advertising and subscription-based models and Internet-based delivery across Microsoft's product line is an important part of what we will do". He revealed that the company plans to add entertainment and Internet services, to its present desktop and server software services. Based on its imminent foray into healthcare, mentioned above, it is clear that the company also plans to add healthcare software services to its product/service mix. Indeed, earlier in July 2006, Kevin Turner, Microsoft's chief operating officer informed a meeting of the firm's business collaborators that the firm is "shifting from being a product-centric company to a services and solutions company". This shift highlights one of the most fundamental issues in software business, one that could determine the success or failure of software companies, namely, the most appropriate business model for software companies, the choice typically between product-and service-centricity, or a mixture of both. These issues are also

14

germane to the contribution of software to ICT GDP, and to a country's overall economy, and to its healthcare delivery. They are also important determinants of competitiveness of the software industry in any country and on the world stage, and considering the effect that business process outsourcing is having on the economy of some developing countries these days, there is no doubt about the need to get the product/service mix right, to attract markets at home and abroad. This underscores the need for determined efforts by both the private and public sector in the realization of these goals, in both promoting research and innovation right from the level of the smaller enterprises that could result in the development of novel and valuable products and services. Considering that, Azyxxi evolved from such efforts by a group of researchers in a not-for-profit hospital many years ago, there is no doubt about the potential of creating the enabling milieu for innovative software product and service development even by the smaller enterprises, which on the aggregate contribute the most to the well being of the economy. There is also no doubt about the need in fact to increase the contributions of both ICT products and service. Actually, both are complementary and their contributions to the economy should increase parri passu. This is more so in the health sector, where the increasing tendency is for both to work together in a constitutive rather than merely in an enabling mode. It is important for example for software, wireless and telecommunications equipments firms to work in tandem in the development of innovative health services, such as wireless diagnostic and even treatment services. There can be no gainsaying the prospects of such services for facilitating the achievement of the dual healthcare goals, for example, in the monitoring of the gait and movement of the elderly hence preventing falls, and in securing help promptly in the event of a fall or a medical event such as heart attack. The recent strategic partnership between Microsoft Corp. and Toronto network equipment provider Nortel Networks attests to the need for such intersectoral collaboration. With the two companies coalescing their core competencies, Microsoft's desktop applications

15

and Nortel's telephone systems, in a four-year agreement, to develop innovative products and services that an organization they formed, the Innovative Communications Alliance, would market, we could expect to see the sort of high quality constitutive products and services in the health sector that it increasingly needs. These products and services would be able to compete favorably in the global markets, boosting Canada's exports growth, besides being fundamental drivers of internal market growth in the local healthcare ICT sector, and of the emergence of a new era of qualitative, client-focused healthcare delivered efficiently and cost-effective by the country's Medicare. Microsoft and Nortel for example plan to collaborate on product development, each licensing the other's technology, marketing the combined products developed in conjunction with each other. Nortel intends to transform the conventional business phone system into a software value proposition, a shift away from just being a product, software included. With the wide range of services yearning for fulfillment in the health sector, the opportunities for this duo to deliver innovative products and services are truly immense. However, they might fail to tap maximally into these vast market resources if they did not fully understand the workings of the country's health system, and the undercurrent waves threatening to bubble to the surface in the near future, some of whose ripples the health system is in fact already feeling. In other words, from a strategic perspective, and in the best interests of all concerned, healthcare ICT companies need to appreciate fully the issues involved in the healthcare sector. For examples, they need to be familiar with issues such as the ongoing private v. public health system debate in the country, the rising health spending, the hospital wait-times issues, and physician availability, remuneration and distribution issues, among others. A cursory look at issues on this list might prompt some to ask what their relevance to Microsoft or Nortel is. However, more in-depth exploration would reveal the underlying issues and their processes and the significant effect they have not just on the quality of healthcare delivery in the country, but also on its escalating costs, both of which could inspire the sort of constitutive products and services mentioned earlier aimed at modifying in a positive way, these issues and processes. Such a process cycle analysis is an important, if not mandatory exercise that these companies and others, both local and foreign, keen to do business in Canada, including investing in its healthcare industry, would need to embark upon in an increasingly competitive business milieu. To highlight this point, not even Microsoft is immune from competition. Its purchase of Azyxxi mentioned earlier is fueling speculation among industry analysts of an imminent showdown between Microsoft and Google, in the long-awaited battle between the two software companies for the health care search and service markets. With Microsoft indicating that, it has formed an alliance with MedStar, developers of Azyxxi, to create collaborative health care applications, there is no doubt that Microsoft has in fact arrived on the healthcare ICT scene, the marketing of its health care ventures probably via the much-speculated Windows Live Healthcare service. Furthermore, its present health site, MSN Health, is gaining increasing traction in the health search domain, with about 6 million visitors each month, a 27% growth since 2005, and something over which Google, which also has strong interests in the healthcare markets, would likely ponder. Indeed, as the company's co-founder, Sergey Brin recently noted, "The first thing that we've done was a part of the launch of Google Co-op, where we improved the quality of our health search." He also said, "More broadly, we've seen that health information has a lot of similarities to the kinds of challenges we deal with in terms of just textual information. So we would like to make sure that for this important issue to many people around the world, of health, that we're actually able to contribute our technology to solve some of those problems". The need to identify the problems and seek the appropriate solutions to them would, indeed make the difference between success and failure in the future of a software company, and indeed, a healthcare ICT company, in the Canadian healthcare ICT industry.

In Canada, with exports of ICT goods falling by 1% in the first 2006 quarter in

Canada versus a 1.4% decline in overall of the country's goods, although long-term, exports of Canadian ICT goods is positive, having increased 29% since a low in the fourth 2003 quarter, much more needs done to prevent another fall next quarter and beyond. This is so, in particular regarding electronic components and computer equipment, with the most losses, exports falling by 11.9% and 12.4%, respectively[2] since the first 2003 quarter, declining incrementally, currently 6.8% below the level of the first quarter of 2003. There was an increase in the exports of communications equipment by 5.4%, with 13.2% increase in wired equipment counterbalancing a 9.7% fall in wireless equipment. These figures underscore the point made earlier about the need for these products to grow also, in order to make the goal of product improvements, for example increasingly fast and innovative chips, inspiring innovative services and vice versa resulting in the operations of both in the constitutive mode crucial to reaping in full their benefits, in healthcare delivery, realizable. Consider the following as an example of what such dyadic symbiosis could achieve. An IST-funded project, called DICOEMS, has come up with a wireless technology platform that make it possible for doctors in hospital ERs to treat remotely, victims of accidents, and other emergencies[4]. It is not news that many such victims lose their lives in locations lacking in the necessary expertise to treat their conditions, or because they could not get to the hospital ER quick enough, and there are many such locations in Canada, particularly in remote and inaccessible areas with limited medical resources. This system, which has specially equipped handheld computers or smart phones, could help solve the problem, save many lives or reduce morbidities, thus not just improving the quality of care delivery, but also saving healthcare costs that would otherwise have gone into the protracted treatment and rehabilitation of some of these accident victims. The system enables paramedics and other emergency personnel first on the scene to send images and crucial patient information, including vital sings data for examples pulse, respiration, and ECG, to experts ER doctors at the hospital's ER department, who are able to monitor the patient's condition via streaming video from the ambulance. The ER experts are therefore able to diagnose and treat the patient including giving the paramedics details of the necessary medical procedures to carry out. No wonder, that Matteo Colombo, a technical specialist at Synergia 2000, the Milan-based project coordinator asserted, "DICOEMS could significantly improve survival rates for victims of accidents or other medical emergencies by reducing the chance of inappropriate treatment...The system will improve decision support, diagnosis and risk management in critical situations occurring far from hospital emergency rooms". This system exemplifies the multidimensional technology convergence that would characterize the healthcare ICT arena in the near future, systems that would not only facilitate the communication and sharing of patient data and information, for example, but would also enable more-constructive use of this veritable information base. Again, Colombo noted, "We found out that there was a big gap in how medical information from an emergency was stored, so emergency-intervention data was not followed up on properly and not available to other health-care providers. This is especially a problem if the patient has a recurring condition". Using a Grid network management system to integrate proficiently geographically dispersed and often-disparate databases, DICOEMS, for example, could in an emergency with the patient in danger, enable patient identification, and access to their recent medical history, before the ambulance reaches the ER, including via the system's multi-channel milieu, the patient's GP being able to participate remotely in the treatment process. The system's global positioning system (GPS) enables central emergency systems to check an ambulance's location, and guide the driver via the quickest and shortest route to the patient's location, and from there to the hospital. Another important feature of the system is that central switchboard operators have access to a text-search tool for searching a specialized database, in order to match the patient's clinical data with the hospital with the best resources to treat the patient's problems, to which they could then inform the ambulance driver to take the patient. The operators simply need to type the relevant keywords describing say and orthopedic emergency, and the system returns the best-equipped hospitals to treat the patient, and their availability at that moment. It is no doubt easy to see the benefits to patients that these technologies offer, and their cost savings potential for Medicare in Canada. Also as important it exemplifies the sort of competition that the Canadian healthcare ICT industry is going to confront increasingly on the global ICT stage, which underscores the need for an intersectoral collaboration to boost the technological and management base of the industry in Canada. We could achieve the former via a determined effort at providing the necessary R&D funds to institutions, research organizations, firms, even individuals, in effect creating the right atmosphere for creativity to flourish, and the latter, ditto, recognizing the important interrelationship between them. The DICOEMS project even attempted to develop and refine a portable polymerase chain reaction device that could analyze patients' blood for DNA, to match against a huge database, which would enable the identification of a comatose patient and access the patient's medical history. However, "...the European Union does not yet have a legal framework allowing collection of an extensive DNA database from the general public. That lack made this goal unworkable. This turned out be the project's biggest obstacle," lamented Colombo, a clear research gap that Canadian researchers could fill for example, making the system more constitutive, and creating opportunities for the Canadian researchers involved a chance to collaborate with the European scientists, and for immense revenue generation from technologies that would feature prominently in patient management in the foreseeable future. According to Colombo, "One possible way we could bridge the problem is to focus on smaller groups, such as firemen or policemen, which could have their own DNA databases. Privacy concerns might be less of an issue, because the organization would manage its own database, which could be used for identifying injured or dead policemen or firemen, for example," the success of which we might add, could inspire the wider applications of the technologies in other segments of society and indeed, in all in the long run. Billed to be in operations by Italian ambulance centers by the end of 2006, with approval by local authorities, the European Commission has also shown interest in these technologies, whose widespread adoption by EU member states would become a potential entry barrier to ER technologies by ICT firms of lower grades. With Canada's increasingly looking across the Atlantic for ICT markets, our ICT firms need to be wary of these and similar developments, a point that highlights an earlier point about the need for process cycle analyses of at least the markets of interest. This is a necessary prelude to formulating the appropriate strategic product/service mix on the one hand and the approaches to scale and scope economies for these markets, on the other.

The example of the DICOEMS shows that software and indeed, other ICT companies need to be proactive and that they could develop innovative products and service that the health sector needs and that would sell remarkably. However, these firms would unlikely be able to meet these market needs ignoring the value of a process cycle analysis where the identification, and decomposition of the issues, both health and non-health, the latter, for example, the issue of legal constraints mentioned above, constitute the crucial starting point for market entry. By yielding other underlying issues and their processes, whose decomposition, yields further even more issues and their processes such analysis would enable the identification of the need for intervention, which could be facilitation, rejection, isolation, or any other, and the appropriate healthcare

ICT to accomplish it. How could the development of such technologies not meet with market success? Further noted Colombo is the need to find partners to exploit the new technology, "In Eastern Europe, since there are no computer-assisted programs like this, DICOEMS could be sold as a whole system. Similar, though less advanced, systems already exist in Western Europe, so these countries could implement modules. DICOEMS is very flexible". Do the investors have to come from Europe? Do these technologies not offer Canadian investors an opportunity to venture into a potential gold mine, literally? Do they also not create opportunities for helping solve some of the country's perennial health problems for example, hospital wait-times, and the chances to reduce hospitalization costs, which guzzle a significant chunk of the country's ever-increasing health spending, while in fact improving the quality of health service provision? Would the country not be achieving the dual healthcare deliver objectives in the process, with the healthcare ICT sector simultaneously contributing to the country's economic growth and sustainable development? Could this not improve the country's productivity and livings standards, hence its GDP per capita, and would this not increase quicker the higher the country's productivity growth, and with living standards higher, would the health and wellbeing not also be, hence productivity increase even higher? Would the country therefore not be achieving its sustainable development goals quicker? Of concern therefore is the country's seemingly persistent problems regarding productivity growth in recent years as figures of the Statistics Canada and US Bureau of Labor Statistics in chart 1 reveals[5, 6].

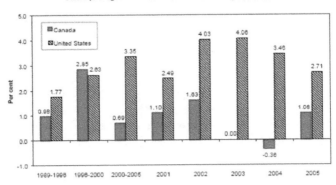

Chart 1: Business Sector Output per Hour Growth in Canada and the United States (average annual and annual rates of change, per cent)

Sources: Statistics Canada and US Bureau of Labor Statistics.

Even with business sector output per hour, the most commonly used gauge of aggregate labor productivity increasing from -0.4% in 2004 to 1.1% in 2005, indicating a potential positive labor growth pattern, this pattern compares unfavorably with the latter part of the previous decade. It has also not compared favorably with that of the U.S lately, which has been on the rise from the first quarter of 2004, (131.7) until that of 2006 (138.9)[7]. It is pertinent to ask why business sector output per hour annual growth rate between 1996 and 2000 of 2.9% fell to 1.1% in 2005, less than half of the figure for the U.S. in the same year, whose average annual rate increases over the past five years have been almost five times that of Canada[8]. What is responsible for the country's labor productivity slump since the start of this decade, a pattern applicable in fact, to the entire country's labor productivity growth that even the marginal labor productivity growth attributable to the non-business, public administration, health, and education, during the same period, could not conceal[8]? Experts have

23

blamed a number of factors for these developments including the decline in capital investment rates, which underscores the points made earlier about the need for intersectoral and collaborative efforts to invest in, for example the semi-conductor sector, and create the enabling environment for the development of innovative constitutive healthcare ICT products and services. This would not only bolster the contribution of the healthcare ICT, but also that of the health industry to Canada's sustainable economic development. To be sure, the country's ICT sector is a major employer of labor in the country as chart 2 below shows, although growth rates declined to 2.4% in 2004, for example, versus 5.3% in 2003. Although the software and computer services industries have been the major contributors to employment in the ICT sector, as noted earlier, it was not much the software part than the other, which means that we need to continue to find ways to improve software business, particularly considering the economy of the country increasingly becoming service-oriented.

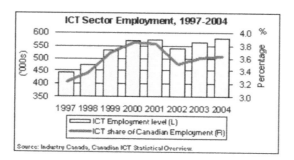

Chart 2: Source: Industry Canada, Canadian ICT Statistical Overview

It is also important to improve this sector not just domestically, but like its

manufacturing partner that has always been predominantly export-oriented, also

24

seek export dominance for Canadian software in the global market, and in particular healthcare software. These efforts could no doubt diminish the sometimes-significant trade deficits that the country has experienced over the years in particular with ICT manufacturing, which increased for example from $8.4 billion to $19.9 billion between 1990 and 1998. Exports of communications equipment have been increasing overall, by 48% since the fourth quarter of 2001, of instruments up 1.0% in the first 2006 quarter. However, as the country's export partners increasingly become more global, so would likely be the intensity of competition. This would place a greater demand on these products to be not just of higher quality, but also to be constitutive. This is why the country cannot afford to ignore the need for the sort of intersectoral collaborative efforts to address the issue concerning the development of these technologies in order to offer such potentially-valuable value propositions as the markets, in particular the healthcare delivery markets, both in Canada, and overseas, would increasingly demand. Canadian ICT is increasingly venturing outside its traditional North American exports domain into the global markets, the EU-25, Russia, and countries in the Middle East, Africa, and Latin America, in particular Brazil, within its strategic orbit, exports to the EU-25, and Russia and these other markets increasing by 22% and 54%, respectively, since the second 2002 quarter. Both groups constituted about a quarter Canadian ICT exports in the first 2006 quarter, those to Asia-Pacific increasing, by 60% since the first quarter of 2002, although fell 10% in the first 2006 quarter. This fall is significant and we should prevent it enduring considering that, roughly, two-thirds of ICT products manufactured in the country are for exports, which increased in 2005, by 8.8%, 5.2% ($22.6 million) of total merchandise exports, mostly of wired (+20.4%) and wireless (+16.9%) communications equipment, both constituting a third of all the country's ICT products exported. Less of these products now go to the U.S., a fall from $31.3 to $15.4 billion, between 2000 and 2005, or 83.9% to 68.2%, whereas exports to the Asia-Pacific rose in 2005, $2.7 billion, or to 12.1% of exports of ICT goods from 4.9% in 2000, and to EU countries, in 2005, $3.1 billion or 13.6% , versus 8.7% in 2000. These figures raise a number of important issues for software and its contribution to the Canadian economy, an increasingly service-based economy, not to mention healthcare software, which, as we noted earlier, has the potential to contribute much more in a variety of ways, more so as the country increasingly ventures outside its traditional export zone. It is instructive for example that the U.S, which is already the major trading partner with the Association of South East Asian Nations (ASEAN) namely, Brunei, Burma, Cambodia, Indonesia, Laos, Malaysia, Philippines, Singapore, Thailand, and Vietnam, signed an inclusive trade agreement with these countries at their July 2006 meeting in Kualar Lumpur. In the agreement, ASEAN and the US agreed on a master plan to foster ASEAN-US relations and cooperation for the next five years (2006-2011). ASEAN Foreign Ministers and US Secretary of State Condoleezza Rice signed the Framework Document for the Plan of Action to Implement the ASEAN-US Enhanced Partnership on 27 July 2005, after the ASEAN Post Ministerial Conference with the US. The Plan covers several issues regarding political and security, economic and social and development cooperation, with 28 sub-areas outlining 161 joint measures and activities, among which is cooperation on preventing, controlling and reducing the impact of communicable and pandemic diseases. With ASEAN countries moving steadily toward forming a European-style Community, having signed a declaration to establish a free trade area by 2020 in an effort to counterbalance the low-wage competition and huge markets of India and China, ASEAN promises to be a potential huge market for Canada's healthcare ICT products and services. Nonetheless, it also poses major competition issues between Canadian and U.S, and calls for the need for the former to establish and strengthen bi-and multi-lateral trade links with these countries. This would be a major chance for Canada to offset some of its significant trade deficits in ICT manufacturing in particular and position its ICT services industries to benefit from the growing economic muscle of these hitherto predominantly agriculture-based but increasingly sophisticated and industrialized economies. To be certain, this deficit fell recently, by 3.8% in 2005 as exports increased faster than imports, although at $20.9 billion, it was still 22.0% more than the 1997 deficit, $17.2 billion, the culprits in 2005, computer equipment, 45%, audio and video equipment, 25%, and electronic components, 20% as chart 3 below shows.

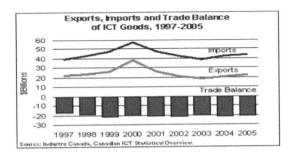

Chart 3: Source: Industry Canada. Canadian ICT Statistical Overview

Could the sort of focus on developing software and other ICT that serve constitutive rather than mere enabling functions, and that could give Canadian firms the edge to compete successfully with U.S, European and from other places worldwide help reduce these deficits perhaps substantially? The point here that now that Canada is exploring Asian markets more aggressively, should its software firms not be ready to take on an ever more competitive global market, and considering the important role that they could play in reducing the country's trade healthcare ICT trade deficits, should we not be seeking to improve the performance of the software industry? Does the Canadian software industry not have much to offer not just ASEAN but other Asian countries for examples, China, and India, with a combined population of almost 2.5 billion peoples, not to mention the erstwhile Tiger economies, which are still in the main buoyant and offer potential lucrative healthcare software markets? Would ASEAN countries, which want to counterbalance the burgeoning economic power of China and India, not create more favorable investments climate, to attract some of the investments now heading for India and China? Could Canadian software firms not exploit these opportunities to offer the investments no doubt essential for South East Asia's development, and from which the firms could reap ample rewards in both the short-and long-terms? An important point to note regarding the agreement between ASEAN and the U.S mentioned above is that a remarkable increase in American investment in China has led to, in the past a steady fall in US funds for South East Asia, a trend that would likely continue if ASEAN did not quickly amalgamate its disparate economies. This is more so considering its mix of relatively rich countries such as Malaysia, poor ones such as Laos, monarchies such as Brunei, and military-ruled such as Burma, not to mention traditional socio-political preferences that could inhibit modern free-market operations. Yet, we should see a speeding up of political reforms and labor and tax laws reforms. They would also have to establish the necessary instruments to attract foreign investment and facilitate international trade, if they were to achieve their goals of catching up with China and India in the stipulated target date of 2020, which in fact the wealthier among them such as Thailand and Singapore even want to fast forward. These developments are likely to create incentives for software and healthcare ICT firms in Canada for example, to exploit these massive markets, for example of China and ASEAN, 1.7billion strong, , even other Asian countries as both along with Japan and India, for example, also recently signed a separate agreement on cooperation in several areas. There are of course market opportunities for Canadian software companies in other parts of the world, in for examples, Europe, Australia, New

Zealand, and indeed, Africa, the latter its healthcare software markets potentially massive, yet relatively untapped. The point then is that Canadian software firms in particular, and other healthcare ICT services firms, have the potential to contribute much more to the country's economic well being than they are currently doing, developing innovative healthcare ICT service packages for both the domestic and international markets, and of course, make profits in the process. They stand a better of doing so, however, crafting a novel approach to the markets that is not just both product and service based, which itself is nothing new, but whose strength lies in its creating this mix based on a thorough process cycle analysis of intended markets, the outcome, an integral part of corporate strategy for any particular market. They should also be able to exploit both scale and scope economies maximally in product/service differentiation, and in acquisition/merger choices, all predicated on the strategic intent emanating from the aforementioned process cycle analysis, for example, to beat wait-times in Canada. In other words, the benchmark would not always, although could, as in the case of Microsoft and Google, on the one hand, and indeed, the former's erstwhile business partners already entrenched in the health industry on the other, be another firm, presumably the industry leader, and could be an issue, part of the outcome-bound health processes the analysis revealed. Again, as is the case with Microsoft and the software Azyxxi, competition could give way to collaboration, as each partner brings to the table a wealth of expertise that the other lacks, creating a more-perfect whole. No doubt, these issues should also inform these firms in venturing onto the international stage, as they enhance their chances of success. Consider one for example that clearly understands the increasing interests in the health sector for wireless technologies. Why would Canadian software and other healthcare ICT firms want to ignore experts' projections for example that global healthcare markets' spending mobile hardware, software, and services would be almost US$3 billion in just fours years time, or surveys indicating that 50% of hospitals noted that wireless technologies are the top emerging technologies in healthcare delivery. There would also be increasing spending on patient management systems in particular with more-widespread diffusion of electronic health records (EHR) technologies, which would in turn, be important in the increased use of wireless technologies, and of electronic prescribing. This is more so in the latter case, for example, as health systems move towards not just rational but safe prescribing, hence markets opening at least in most countries in the developed world for these products and services. Yet, Canadian firms also need to know the issues peculiar to the use of these technologies, for examples, bandwidth and interoperability issues in order to be able to target the right package of products and services at the right markets, and competitively. This particular point is crucial considering the criticisms by some of electronic health records (EHR) for example that it is uncertain that these technologies would reduce healthcare costs or improve care, according to a recent article published in the July/August issue of the journal Health Affairs[10]. In particular the author contended that EHR could actually result in increased billing, reduce doctors' productive and does not change provider-to-patient ratios. These observations are not in fact new. As the author Jaan Sidorov, MD, an associate in the department of general internal medicine at Geisinger Medical Center, in Danville, Pa. himself observed, "Absent other fundamental interventions that alter medical practice, it is unlikely that the U.S. health care bill will decline as a result of the EHR alone." This is the key point. Besides the fact that the author acknowledged that he did not design the study to examine all the arguments in favor of EHR, and that he conducted it in just ambulatory care, the study actually underscores one of the major points that we have made in our discussion thus far. This is regarding the need for software and other healthcare ICT to be constitutive rather than being simply conceptualized as enabling. In other words, for a thorough understanding of all the issues involved and the role that these technologies could play literally "embedded" in these issues in the quest for improved outcome. Thus, we could only reap the benefits of EHR and indeed, other healthcare ICT by conceptualizing these technologies this way, and as other studies have shown, most users of EHR have not installed some of the advanced functions expected to bring improvements in care and reduced costs. This highlights the issues concerned with healthcare ICT diffusion that also need addressing in order for the full economic and health benefits of these technologies to materialize.

Why would a healthcare provider expect to enjoy the benefits of uninstalled features of the technologies would be one question, but why would the provider not install these features in the first place, another. There are also issues of upgrading the software to make them more efficient and not reduce rather than enhance doctors' productivity an issue whose underlying processes that need modifying software firms, if they would embrace the concept of process cycle analysis mentioned earlier should be able to identify and rectify. In other words, this is one of many issues that Canadian software firms could develop the appropriate software solutions for, the market clearly potentially huge. Furthermore, although, and as the author of the study noted, EHRs could help facilitate pay-for-performance programs and management of chronically ill patients, deriving full benefits from EHRs, requires among others, system changes. These changes should predicate on a clear understanding of the relevant issues, health, and nonhealth, whose interplay results in the outcome, namely healthcare delivery, the quality of which, the measures taken following this process cycle analysis, would determine. Besides being counter-intuitive to consider that conceptualizing software and other healthcare ICT as constitutive rather than as merely a utility would not have a positive influence on healthcare delivery and reduce health spending, several studies have indeed, acknowledged these benefits, including a recent one by the Rand Corp. The study found that national adoption of the EHRs in the U.S could result in over $81 billion in annual savings. There is also no doubt about the potential of healthcare software and other technologies to reduce medical errors and save lives, attributes that even if quantifiable, are simply priceless. A recent report in the journal Pediatric Care medicine for example observed that an online infusion calculator and a computerized ordering system for drug treatment and other types of intravenous infusion significantly reduce the risk of medication errors in children. On comparing handwritten and calculator-generated orders, the authors found error rates of 45 and 6 errors per every 100 hundred orders written, respectively. These results clearly indicate that Web-based calculator reduces the likelihood of ordering and giving a child the wrong medication dose or other errors for example leaving out patient information or inserting the wrong one, as the calculator stops ordering errors prior to reaching the pharmacist let alone the child. Developed by Christopher Lehman and his team at the John Hopkin's Children Center in the U.S, has been in use now for three years, the calculator computes medication doses, advises, and alerts doctors to medication interactions, and automatically proffers default doses and medication dilutions, to prevent under-and over-dosing. It is unlikely that the answers to queries about the potential of this technology to reduce both the health and economic burden of medication errors would be far to seek. Again, as this technology demonstrates, a key consideration in developing software and other healthcare ICT is what the issues involved in healthcare delivery are, be they as regard a task, such as medication administration, or the functioning of an entire health system. Without such in-depth understand, it would be difficult if not impossible to develop the most appropriate solutions that would lead to the realization of the dual healthcare delivery objectives mentioned above. It would also be difficult for a software firm to be and/or remain competitive and profitable, as its competitors that engaged in process cycle analysis would have more-acceptable products on the market. Then there are issues surrounding the technologies themselves, for example, even the most basic step in developing information systems, accurate and inclusive documentation structured in architectures, which would facilitate access and interoperability, could be fraught with difficulties. This is besides some critical issues such as person identity matching, validation of upstream system-data quality validation, and clinical record identity, among others, essential for system interoperability and the successful implementation of a National Health Information System. There are also issues of standardization, of clinical terminologies and of technical standards, business rules, policies and procedures, and of implementation directives that are important to consider in health data and information exchange projects, and to support software applications' interoperability, including in EHRs. Continuity of Care Records, the Health Level Seven (HL7) messaging standard, the HL7 clinical data architecture, the HL7 EHR functional model, and SNOMED CT, are some of the many messaging and content standards in EHRs currently. It is important not only to know the terminologies for standardizing data and information communication and sharing in an EHR, in the market of interests, for example, healthcare software firms also should know nature and extent of the need for related products and services in these markets. Thus, they should know these needs regarding interoperability via content mapping between disparate systems, for example of SNOMED CT to U.S administrative code sets (ICD-9CM, and CPT, for examples), which would facilitate healthcare provider documentation to billing processes' connection, and could help with reimbursement, epidemiology and other issues. There could also be issues that would require outsourcing due to staffing shortages, lack of the required expertise or technologies, even costs, that healthcare software firms ought to be able to identify in their target markets, as they should be able to, the needs that would arise thereof, for example for educational programs' software. The point is that without embracing the concept of process cycle analysis or identifying the issues and the required solutions some way else, that would improve healthcare delivery quality in their markets of interest, and which, for Medicare, and indeed, for all healthcare stakeholders, would curtail health spending, their market penetration, and indeed, competitiveness, would be defective. Canadian healthcare software firms ought to adopt a different mindset that aims to develop innovative product/service mixes capable of transforming the entire health system for the better, not necessarily in one fell swoop, but of its components parts albeit incrementally as the system forges ahead in its relentless path towards increasingly higher quality. This journey would be, of necessity, never ending, as no health system could ever be perfect. This is simply because the system is constantly undergoing changes some of which, for example, the outbreak of an unanticipated event such as bioterrorism via a previously unknown killer-bug, could be disruptive to a more or less extent for system functioning and cohesion. These changes might therefore, introduce new issues that require decomposition and exposition to understand their full ramifications, and underlying processes, revelations that could warrant further decomposition, and exposition, in a perpetual motion of process cycle analysis. In any case, even without such unanticipated event, subjecting the health system to ongoing performance evaluation and quality assurance and control, would ensure its continuing efficiency and cost-effectiveness and sustainable improvement. This in itself is inherent in the underlying assumptions regarding the contributions that the health sector could make to the overall economy of the country. Without the quality of the health system being as high as it always could, it would remain a constant drain on the country's economy, requiring as it currently does, an increasing percentage of the GDP to fund, and even more disturbing, possibly without still making any significant effect on many of the major issues confronting the health system. As we have seen, this discussion also elaborates on the symbiotic relationship between health and economy, the need for this relationship to yield a positive outcome for both, and the role that the software industry in Canada could play in that regard. This contribution incidentally dipped in the first quarter of 2006 as earlier noted also as Figure 3 shows, improvements in the contributions of other ICT services industries in fact, also desirable.

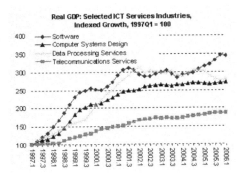

Figure 3: Source: strategis.ic.gc.ca[1]

In other words, by improving its performance both at home and in foreign markets, the industry could be helping Canada achieve the dual healthcare delivery goals, and sustainable economic development, the industry in the process attaining high levels of proficiency, and profitability. Both of these would make it even more competitive, hence better able to make even more contributions to the country and to its members' bottom-line. On the home front for example, for software there are still immense business openings where rectifying the information asymmetry that has plagued the health industry, albeit rooted in atavistic paternalism, could be of interest, and should considering the relative use of the Internet and web presence in the health sector versus education and arts as chart 4 shows. Even if these figures relate to private enterprises, when they would be even more telling, as this sector has more compelling business reasons to be out there on the Internet or to use it, they suggest the characteristic lag by an information-intensive industry in the use of health information technologies compared to others, not even so information-intensive sectors. Witness the imminent if not already ongoing health-sector search engine race between Google and Microsoft, evidence that some software firms have identified the myriad of business opportunities that healthcare information provision and knowledge management offer, an opportunity that is wide open to Canadian software firms, too.

Internet use and presence of Web sites						
	2003	2004	2005	2003	2004	2005
	Enterprises that use the Internet			Enterprises with a Web site		
	%					
Educational services (private sector)	92.9	94.4	96.8	71.6	77.7	82.9
Health care and social assistance (private sector)	77.7	83.2	84.3	21.8	26.0	26.4
Arts, entertainment and recreation	86.8	88.9	91.1	51.6	53.0	59.3

Chart 4: Source: Statistics Canada[11]

Besides the Internet, software companies could develop products of the constitutive type mentioned earlier that would not only be able to deliver targeted and contextualized health information to say subscribers wherever and whenever, for example, but in a truly transformational manner be able to advice on the measures that need taken under certain circumstances based on progress in medical knowledge. For examples, it might be able to offer options regarding what types of health information to subscribe to based on learned user preferences, or whether to continue to take a certain vitamin in light of new scientific research indicating it does not work for the particular reason the individual was taking the vitamin. In our increasingly action-packed and fast-paced world, and more suave healthcare clientele, the demand for sophisticated and interactive healthcare products and services would likely increase, creating significant market opportunities for software companies that able to read their target markets accurately and to incorporate what they found in multi-level strategic initiatives. The increasing tendency toward private health services provision in Canada would also likely heighten this increased sophistication in the demand for health services as competing healthcare providers jostle for clients, who become more discerning in the disposition of their healthcare dollars. These providers would need to impress clients with differentiated and more advanced products and services, via healthcare information and communication technologies, the most likely candidates for a wide range of primary, secondary, and tertiary prevention services, pricing likely falling as the push from commoditization of these technology-based become increasingly intense. Again, it is unlikely that a Canadian healthcare software firm that has done its process cycle analysis for one or more of these services would likely miss the opportunity to develop, perhaps in collaboration with other firms, the appropriate healthcare software to meet the needs for these value-added services. Software firms would find niche markets even at the high-end of service provision that is specialty service lines or what an article in Health Affairs on July 25, 2006 termed the medical arms race[12], with the sprouting of heart and cancer centers, orthopedic hospitals, and other niche specialty "centers of excellence". This phenomenon, on the rise in the U.S, and in Canada the authors of this article noted indicates intensification in a novel medical arms race with healthcare providers developing and marketing often high-tech-based, specialty-service lines. These establishments would not only need to compete with one another, but also with hospitals that traditionally provide such services, on the basis of cutting-edge diagnostic and treatment capabilities, they would also need to embrace the increasing desire of a more discerning healthcare clientele for health promotion and disease prevention services. Besides software being an integral part of the high-tech medical technologies that they utilize, creating business avenues for Canadian software firms at every phase of the software development lifecycle, they would also find business openings developing and maintaining software for these other value propositions. This is another aspect of the future of the healthcare software tied with developments in the health industry, hence the need for the sort of process cycle analysis mentioned earlier. Thus, whether the trend toward private health service provision would spread in Canada, as it is already legal to some extent in Quebec and some provinces have indicated their interest in allowing it to varying degrees, its nature, and extent would be key determinants of the future of not just the health, but also the healthcare software industry in Canada. These issues in other words, would be crucial to changes in the contribution of the software industry, and indeed, the entire healthcare ICT sector to the economic growth and sustainable development of the country. The details of how the dynamics of the interplay between the private and public health sectors would play out in all its aspects would be in the main conjectural barring equally in-depth process cycle analysis of each of the key issues involved, the complexity, yet necessity of which supports the need for an incremental-type process cycle analysis approach. This way, decomposed issues would yield underlying issues and their processes with further decomposition yielding new exposition ad infinitum, the appropriate healthcare software and other ICT identified and applied as the process evolves. Suffice to say though, and as the proliferation of specialty-line practices mentioned above shows, these practices would be in keen competition for clients with government hospitals, the result of which might be a dramatic change in the status of government hospitals, as we know them today. Specifically, and as these government hospitals find it increasingly difficult to justify their provision of specific services, or the very existence of their entire facilities due to marked reduction in clientele, service utilization, yet increasing maintenance costs for example, some might merge with others, outsource certain services, or even shut down. These developments, again, with a clear understanding of the issues involved would generate fertile grounds for software companies to do business, depending on the outcome of their analyses of the pressing of and the most appropriate product/service mix for the markets in question. As these software firms would also be competing with local, and indeed, foreign software and ICT firms, time would be of the essence in conducting such analyses and incorporating their outcomes into strategic intents. Lurking in the background its effect in both domestic and foreign markets for Canadian software potentially massive is the issue of open source software, in particular for those Canadian software firms looking to explore Latin America's, especially, Brazil's, healthcare software markets. The issue of desktop versus web-based applications such as customer relations management (CRM) solutions would also become important as the competition for clients in the health sector intensifies and the need for offering sophisticated client experience cost-effectively gains increasing traction in management circles in the health sector. There a variety of other issues, that would be important for healthcare software firms to consider in the build up of their interests in healthcare markets both at home and in competing in the international arena. Such considerations would stand the firms in better stead to achieve their profit objectives in both the short and long-terms. They would also facilitate the ability of the industry as a whole to increase its contribution to Canada's economy. It would be doing so by contributing to that of the health sector to achieve its dual healthcare delivery goals, which on the aggregate would increase the country's productivity, reduce its need to spend more of health even further, making resources available for other sectors of the economy such as education, social services, and maintaining law and order. These developments would create an enabling setting for further development and more sustainable economic growth, all of which in turn would benefit the health software industry. The industry would not only keep reaping the rewards of its strategic investments in the local economy, it would also become more competitive abroad. It would be able to develop innovative products and services for its exports markets and even better endowed with increasing numbers of highly talented corp. of software engineers and managers, which the increased investments by the country in educating its youths for example, would likely bring. An interconnection between various components of Canadian economy is thus crucial to the future of software business in Canada. Making these relationships, work for positive developments in the country's economy is an urgent task that confront us all and that we must achieve.

References

1. Available at: http://strategis.ic.gc.ca/epic/internet/inict-tic.nsf/print-en/h_it06100e.html
Accessed on July 26, 2006

2. Available at:
http://www.nytimes.com/2006/07/26/technology/26cnd-soft.html?_r=1&ref=technology&pagewanted=print&oref=slogin
Accessed on July 27, 2006

3. Available at:
http://news.com.com/Ballmer+Software+is+becoming+a+service/2100-1012_3-6099198.html
Accessed on July 27, 2006

4. Available at:
http://istresults.cordis.lu/index.cfm/section/news/tpl/article/BrowsingType/Features/ID/82873
Accessed on July 28, 2006

5. Available at: http://cansim2.statcan.ca/cgi-win/cnsmcgi.exe?Lang=E&ResultTemplate=Srch2&CORCmd=GetTList&CORId=2621
Accessed on July 28, 2006

6. Rao, Someshwar, Andrew Sharpe and Jeremy Smith (2005) "An Analysis of the Labor Productivity Growth Slowdown in Canada since 2000", *International Productivity Monitor*, Number 10, Spring, pp. 3-23.

7. Available at: http://www.bls.gov/news.release/prod2.t01.htm
Accessed on July 28, 2006

8. Available at: http://www.csls.ca/misc/ICP.pdf
Accessed on July 28, 2006

9. Available at: http://strategis.ic.gc.ca/epic/internet/inict-
tic.nsf/en/h_it07229e.html
Accessed on July 28, 2006

10. Available at: http://www.healthcareitnews.com/printStory.cms?id=5218
Accessed on July 29, 2006

11. Available at: http://www.statcan.ca/Daily/English/060420/d060420b.htm
Accessed on July 29, 2006

12. Available at: http://content.healthaffairs.org/cgi/reprint/hlthaff.25.w337v1
Accessed on July 29, 2006

Prospects and Challenges in Canada Healthcare Software Exports

Healthcare software companies in Canada are operating in an increasingly competitive global marketplace. This would create immense opportunities for profitability, but they would also confront challenges of various kinds, their success in the end hinged on their ability to exploit the former, and to overcome the latter. Put differently, that these markets are there is not equivalent to them being for the taking, nor it is that the obstacles they create are insurmountable. A variety of factors are important in how the approaches to either play out eventually, including for example, the strategic orientation of these firms, the operating institutional climate in Canada, and in the intended export market, progress in medical knowledge, and advances in healthcare information and communication technologies, among others. It would be important for example if a software firm chose a vertical or niche market or opted for a horizontal market, as the former attempting to address the specialized needs of specific domains of the healthcare sector, the latter, its more general needs, would confront different issues, that could significantly impact the business outcome for either firm. Firms that operate in niche markets for example often market pricier products and services for restricted markets in competition, typically stiff, with other firms, marketing similar products and services designed to solve identical problems, and often not available to the general public. Those that operate in horizontal markets typically develop more generic and less costly, products and services often for a wider consumer base, for example, word processors that are useful in all industries, and for the public at large. However, the success or otherwise of

Canadian software firms on the global stage would unlikely be solely dependent on these considerations, as would not even some typical market characteristics, for example, the nature and intensity of the competition that Canadian software firms would face, alone be. For these firms to succeed in the exports markets therefore, they need to be aware of and appreciate fully the numerous factors on the outcome of whose interplay the success of their enterprises depend. This is even more so that the global software market is not just becoming more competitive, but also, more complex, as the demand for products and services become more sophisticated, among both corporate buyers, and individual consumers. This increasing sophistication, fueled by what some would consider the frenetic pace of technological progress, and in the health industry in particular, that of medical progress as well, are crucial determinants of the product and service acquisition. In addition to appreciating the potential influence of challenges for examples technical challenges including standardization and interoperability of disparate systems, and in the health domain, concerns for patient safety, and the security of patient information, creating innovative products and services that could overcome them would be important differentiators for software firms in realization their goals of market capture and dominance. This quest for differentiation would have to be an ongoing exercise, as consumers' increasing panache feeds into the demand for even higher quality differentiators for specific problems, a perpetual challenge that discerning software firms would endeavor to meet, a likely imperative in any case for the survival of any such firm in the near future. It is not that there are no software products to keep children safe surfing the Internet for example. Many such products and services have been around for long. Yet, that children remain and are in fact increasingly unsafe while on the Internet is common knowledge. Would a Canadian software company not be meeting the needs of parents worldwide to safeguard the emotional, even physical health of their children developing software that would make Internet surfing safer for children? The market for such software is potentially huge, but so would competition for it likely be. Thus, for any firm to play big in such a market, it has to differentiate itself from the crowd, literally. Indeed, a virtual ID card recently launched in the U.S., Canada, the UK, and Australia, exemplifies this point. The software, the NetIDMe card, is one that children in chat rooms online, or using instant messaging or social networks could swap, and for which both children and parents could apply, using credit cards and a form countersigned by a professional that knows the child. The idea of the card is to make it more difficult for adults to pose as children online, which would no doubt safeguard children from online predators, a rampant problem, not surprising with, as the Child Exploitation and Online Protection Centre (Ceop) noted, one in twelve of them first meeting someone online[1]. NetIDMe would not work if two children messaging each other online have both not signed up to the scheme, those that have, swapping their assigned NetID nicknames, taking turns to log onto the website of the service. By making it much easier for children to verify the age gender, and general location of someone before choosing to chat with the person, this ID scheme, which also uses software techniques akin to those used by the passport agency to authenticate ID card applications, has no doubt raised the competition bar in the market for such products and services[2]. This is not necessarily a setback as it not only instructs strategic intent, but also inspires creativity and innovation, for example, in the development of authentication technologies for the health sector. Such novel, ironclad technologies would not only garner immense patronage they would make a significant a difference to public confidence in the ability of health information and communication technologies to ensure the privacy of health information, hence embrace them more, fostering the wider diffusion of these technologies, and increasing market opportunities for software firms. Voice over IP (VoIP) technologies are also ongoing development in the ICT industry with the potential for opportunities and challenges for Canadian software firms, even more so as broadband become less expensive, and more pervasive.

Computer users are currently able to make calls over the Internet using these technologies that many noted creates outstanding sound quality, in some cases even free, many also reporting a significant reduction in their phone bills, potentially generating pain or revenue depending on whether the recipient is a telephone company or a software firm, respectively. Telephone companies might be having cognitive dissonance just imagining what would become of them in the near future with the increasing tendency toward first taking the PC out of the VoIP equation as subscribers are able to make internet phone calls via their own cordless handsets. Even more threatening, would be when subscribers could use these handsets outside their homes or offices anywhere, with progress in Wi-Fi technologies, and with for examples, spectrum limitation and authentication issues resolved. Could Canadian software firms not explore solutions to some of these problems for example, those regarding authentication? What are the prospects for such firms filling a yawning market need? There are also now phones using the cellular phone protocol, GSM with incorporated Wi-Fi & VoIP features, which pose a major threat to landline telephones, not to mention WiMax technologies in the near future menacing mobile phone protocols for examples CMDA and UMTS. Could Canadian software firms not collaborate with other ICT firms in developing innovative products and services in anticipation of these future developments? Furthermore, multiple standards-based, converged devices that utilize SIP or UMA, for examples, converged dual-radio handsets are potential mobile phones' competitors, considering their superior spectrum allocation, which would be invaluable with the projected increase in data and voice services and bandwidth demand; in reducing dropped

46

calls' levels, and in prospects for a range of value-added service propositions, among others. Could Canadian software companies not in fact be exploring enhancing UNC authentication of access via dual-radio handset to GSM and GPRS, voice and data services, respectively, over unlicensed wireless networks such as a Wi-Fi wireless LAN? Should they also not be exploring adapting the Spanish start-up, FON model, with users able to share their Wi-Fi bandwidths with others via their personal routers fitted with the appropriate software, enabling users WiFi access outside their homes via other "Fonero" connections, for a fee? Could Canadian software firms not develop innovative software to enhance its adoption, in particular addressing the security issues including the vulnerabilities of the commonest wireless encryption standard, Wireless Equivalent Privacy (WEP) that plague this "peer-to-peer" technology? Would the mushrooming of free wireless networks in many developed countries for example not in fact broaden the scope for a variety of software products and services, including for healthcare delivery in the software markets, including for open source software, which many of these networks use? What are the prospects of developing software specifically for transmitting data/voice healthcare delivery services over these networks, particularly to remote areas with limited access to health services? As noted earlier, these potential market opportunities also come with challenges some unrelated to technical issues, for example, in this case, the potential legal issues involved with sharing Internet connectivity that ISPs could raise. There is therefore need for Canadian software firms to be not just cognizant of the opportunities for product and service development, and indeed, such that they are able to compete favorably in the exports markets, but also of the variety of challenges that could hinder their achievement of these objectives. Many software firms have had to deal with clients' shrinking budgets, even bankruptcies, and have had to institute structural changes to remain afloat, let alone profitable. Many others have had to change their business models, modify their strategies, develop new products, and explore new markets at home and overseas in the face of increasing competition, improve customer satisfaction, and cope with the curtailment of ICT acquisition by their clients. This is not mention, software firms having to prove return on investment (ROI) in order to have their clients, even listen to their propositions. Some firms have also had to downsize and spend less on marketing risking revenue hits that could compound their already complex survival problems, and adopt other cost saving measures to remain in business. These challenges persist for many Canadian software firms today to a more or less extent. The point in fact is that rather than hope to wish them away magically, or some way else, these firms should embrace them as inherent business attributes and strive to overcome them, perhaps even actively seek potential new business opportunities for existing customer development and growth markets for new customer acquisition in the process. Canadian software firms in fact need to embark on more-aggressive geographical expansion campaigns onto the global software stage in general, and for those interested in particular in the health industry, the global healthcare software stage. They need to be able to foray into markets in Europe, Asia, Latin America, and other parts of the world, including the mostly unexplored but huge markets in Africa, and in particular sub-Saharan Africa, to generate new growth markets, while consolidating their market penetration in the U.S. and Mexico. This in itself suggests not just the need to expect a variety of cultural challenges but also the need to develop different marketing strategies, both of which would be difficult if not impossible to achieve without Canadian software firms having a thorough understanding of these markets, or at least of those that interest them. In other words, Canadian software firms need to be able to analyze on an ongoing basis, or have access to such analyses, issues, and developments both in the health and in the software, and indeed, the entire ICT industries, within and outside the country to compete successfully in international markets. Thus, would it not be appropriate for a Canadian software firm to know the nature of the relationship between Canada not only at the trading but also at economic and political levels, and its intended foreign market prior to investing in that market or in a product planned for export to it? Would it not profit from an appreciation of the status of other Canadian firms in technological and trading terms with that market in order to explore opportunities for technical collaboration or joint investments in it? Could such knowledge not inform the firm of the technical sophistication of the technological output of Canada in the internal market that it needs to surpass to start with in and prior to considering exports? These analyses are doubtless, crucial for strategic orienting and planning. Thus, it would be easier for a software firm to determine the most appropriate product/service mix to offer its intended market, for example a country in south east Asia, if it understood fully, the status of that country's health system, and the interplay of the key drivers of its future direction. This is besides the need for the software firm to know its competitors, local and foreign in the healthcare ICT market in the country, the types and quality of the products and services that these other firms are offering, or even plan to offer, and the reception the market gave to these products and services. It is not difficult to see the loss that a software firm could potentially incur not doing its "homework" before venturing into the market, which would amount to reckless adventurism for which there is hardly room in present day increasingly competitive business milieu. Furthermore, the need for Canadian software firms to be more competitive on the global stage has implications not just for their success but also for the economic development of the country, which no doubt, in turn is important for the survival of these firms, in many distinct but important ways. To be sure, the computer services industries, have been doing well regarding the overall Canadian economy, approximately a third of the information and communications technology (ICT) services sector, reporting a significant rise in 2004 revenues, growth in 2002 and 2003, less noticeable, and as opposed to its manufacturing counterpart, ICT services continuing to grow since the 2001 technology slump. Operating revenues for computer systems design and related services, software publishing, and data processing, hosting and related services increased, by 9% to $29.7 billion also in 2004[3]. In the same year, computer systems design and related services, the leader of the three industries, which made a profit overall of $950 million in 2004, had the highest operating revenue increase of 10% from the previous year, operating expenses increasing at a bit higher rate, with an operating profit margin of 5%, a slight decrease from the previous year. The picture for software publishers was not however that rosy, as despite a profit margin of 5% in 2004, due in the main to an increase in operating revenues by 8%, same rate as in 2003, had an operating loss in 2003, with its contribution to the country's GDP actually falling in the first quarter of 2006. Data processing, whose operating revenue growth in 2004 was a mere 1% trailed the other two industries, although its falling operating expenses buoyed its profit margins to 8% in 2004 twice its rate the previous year.

$\mathbf{A}$s noted earlier, Canadian software firms, need to be aware of a variety of

market and industry information in order to plan and executive successful strategies both in markets targeted and in the product/service offerings. The three industries mentioned above for example derived their operating revenue growth from different sources, with computer systems design generating a 25% sales increase from government clients, unlike software publishers, whose government sales actually fell while sales to businesses rose by 14%, with as much as 45% sales share derived from exports. Furthermore, and with regard software publishers, the exports sales might have been a small rise compared to the previous year, but the industry kept up its exports pace relative to other service industries, which is also, why the decline mentioned above for the first quarter of 2006 threatens this pattern. With the country's economic activity

50

remaining in essence fixed in May, increasing 0.1% in March and April, 2006, and for the third month in a row, goods production falling, -0.5% in May, wiping off the gain in services, +0.2%, gains mainly in wholesale trade, the financial sector and public administration, both manufacturing and services need to perform better. Indeed, the ICT monthly gross domestic product at basic prices in chained dollars (1997) has been falling since April 2006, 04%, and 0.2% in May, and June 2006, respectively[4]. Data processing exports and sales to the consumer market increased making up for the sales decline to businesses and governments. Ontario's growth was highest at $1.4 billion, a 10% rise in operating revenues, most from the computer systems design industry, unlike in British Columbia, with a $671 million growth to which all the three industries contributed, software publishers contributing more than 50%. Growth was up in Quebec and Alberta, up $237 million, or 4%, and $131 million, or 5%, respectively, although the data processing industry declined in both and in Manitoba at the rear of the national trend, with operating revenues falling indeed, in all three industries, the overall fall, $91 million or 14%. The contribution of these industries to the country's overall employment rates is also an indicator of their contribution to its overall economic growth and sustainable development. In the period under consideration, employment went up by 7% to 189,000 for three industries, with computer systems ahead with an 11% increase. Software publishing's contribution to employment, although increased, was only by 4%, mostly in British Columbia, data processing recording 2,300 job losses, a 14% decline[3]. The overall growth in employment in the country in 2006 as at July is 1.3% (+210,000), a 0.9% increase over the first seven months of 2005. Employment growth rate in Alberta, +3.9%, is thrice more than the national average, Saskatchewan's next, also an impressive +2.3%, during the same period, Ontario's and British Columbia's just matching the national average[5]. Did the software industry contribute significantly to employment growth in the first seven months of 2006, and indeed, did the ICT industry as whole? During this

51

period, there was strong employment growth in some industries, specifically, natural resources (+5.6%); health care and social assistance (+5.2%); finance, insurance, real estate and leasing (+4.9%) and business, building and other support services (+3.7%)[5]. Clearly, the answers to our earlier questions could not be in the affirmative. In fact, there was a noticeable decline in manufacturing as a whole in the country during this period, an estimated overall fall in July 2006, mostly in Ontario and Quebec, of 33,000, making total losses since the end of 2002, 224,000, or 9.6%[5]. Healthcare ICT as whole and the software industry in particular therefore need to examine ways by which to improve their contribution to Canada's economy in their overall best interests. The contribution of the ICT sector to Canada's employment growth in the 1990s is well known. With one in every six new jobs over the decade created in the ICT sector, and in large cities such as Toronto, Montreal, Vancouver, and Ottawa, four in every ten[6]. Would these companies still have access to the diversity and quality of labor that they did in the cities if there were no jobs to fill in the first place, due for example to these firms moving out to seek lower labor or reduced cost locations in the country or overseas? How could these industries for example have the high-level workers crucial to the continuity of the innovative process crucial to their survival without employing new personnel? How could they hope to compete favorably on the global stage without such potential for creativity and for the development of cutting-edge products and services on an ongoing basis, a lack that could compromise the hoped-for success of the interplay of the country's overall economy and the health of its peoples? Would compromising, the health of its peoples not hinder Canada's efforts at sustainable development, and would this not further compromise the ability of the country to produce and nurture a qualitative workforce, which would diminish economic productivity, the cycle repeating itself ad infinitum? The point here in general terms is the need for the Canadian software industry to recognize the significant role that it has to play in the country's increasingly service-based economy, that this need transcends any altruistic considerations, and that its very survival hinges on it. The ICT sector contributed $55 billion to Canadian GDP in 2003, 5.4% of the country's total economy, a hike from a 4.0% input in 1997. Could the sector continue to make such immense contributions to the economy, and could its appreciation of the need to make such contributions drive its internal reform? Its ability to appreciate fully the issues involved in meeting this need is therefore undeniably crucial, and tied with that of the issues germane to its strategic exports orientation in the short and the long terms. In other words, Canadian software firms need to engage in decomposing these internal and external issues so to say, and with regard the health industry, some of which would be health related and others not, thereby exposing additional underlying issues, in a continuous process cycle analysis. This analysis would serve different purposes depending on what it set out to achieve. One such exercise that aims at moving technology forward for example could have resulted in a project that scientists at The University of Manchester launched recently, seeking to combine web accessibility with cutting-edge mobile phone technologies[7]. The three-year project aims to develop a variety of new software that could make the mobile web just as easy to use as the Internet. At present, websites need redesigning to work on cellular phones because of the difficulty displaying them on small screens, a problem that effectively limits the content available on the mobile web, and one that the RIAM project, intends to solve. The project would take a cue from the experiences of blind and visually impaired users and the technologies they use to surf the internet, such as screenreaders, in order to simplify website content and make them viewable on mobile phone screens. The University of Manchester's School of Computer Science's Dr Simon Harper heads the £205k project that the Engineering and Physical Sciences Research Council funds, in collaboration with Yeliz Yesilada and Professor Ian Horrocks, semantic web and web accessibility experts, respectively. According to Dr Harper, "Mobile web users are handicapped not by physiology but technology. Not only is the screen

53

on the majority of phones very small, limiting the user's vision, but the information displayed is difficult to navigate and read...Add to this the fact that the content displayed is determined by a service provider and not the user and you have a web which is not very accessible or user friendly. Our aim is to change this by enabling web accessibility and mobile technologies to interoperate." A major aspect of the project would be the development of a validation engine that would screen websites to ensure they are accessible and mobile web compatible, the engine working together with a transcoding program that would not only de-clutter web pages but also reorder them into a format that is easy to read on a mobile phone screen. Furthermore, upon decoding, the user would be able to determine the form of page display on the screen, adding Dr Harper, "Screenreaders used by blind or visually impaired web users are very good at stripping web pages down into text only formats, but what we want to achieve are content rich formats which are just as accessible." This project exemplifies the outcome Canadian software firms could expect engaging in the sort of process cycle analysis earlier mentioned. Again, as previously mentioned, the focus of these firms could be on several different issues, all of them critical to the achievement of their strategic objectives. In the health industry for example, most, if not all countries have the need to provide their residents qualitative health services, but with the skyrocketing costs of doing so, and the limited resources often available for this purpose also seek to deliver these services cost-effectively. In other words, these countries want to achieve the dual healthcare delivery goals of providing high quality healthcare while simultaneously reducing their health spending. With this as the starting point, Canadian software companies need then to explore the variety of issues involved in the country that they intend to market their products and services to, which could be hindering the achievement of these objectives, or facilitate the process. In other words, they need to conduct a series of process cycle analyses for these countries, again, based on the particular market segment of interest to them. Such analyses, which they could outsource, if they lacked the human and other resources to perform them, would reveal these issues, further, perhaps even cryptic additional issues, their underlying processes, and in a continuous decomposition/exposition cycle, of course barring any historical fallacy, lay bare potential market opportunities. This would include their characteristics such as market size and competition, and if there are products and services serving them already, and their nature and quality, among others vital information. Considering the aforementioned, what then are the prospects and challenges that Canadian healthcare software firms could expect in the contemporary global market scene and how best could they navigate the increasingly treacherous paths of an equally increasingly hypercompetitive exports markets?

Perhaps what these firms should first want to know is indeed, that competition on the global stage is not becoming easier. Recent developments with some of the biggest players in the ICT industry attest to this. AOL for example, the internet component of Time Warner, and a commercial e-mail technology pioneer, recently announced that it would give away e-mail, instant messaging, software and other services free to high-speed internet users. With shareholder pressure on Time Warner to tap more value from AOL, the company in turn wants AOL to capitalize on the increasing ubiquity of broadband use and online advertising. AOL, in fact and in consequence, no longer keen to market its dial-up service with any remarkable zeal, keener to become an advertising-supported internet network focused on information and entertainment provision[8]. Is it any surprise that this erstwhile Internet leader is changing its business model, considering the stiff competition it faces with other Internet firms for long offering e-mail free? In 2005, AOL offered much of its content, for examples, news, music, and sports information, on its website gratis, and has since been exploring moving to a new model offering free services, such as Google or Yahoo's services, with its eye on luring advertisers to its fold. In fact, the company's advertising revenue has been on the rise, up 40% from 2005, and although it also lost 976,000 subscribers versus the first quarter, its 26.7 million subscribers in September 2002, down by over 25% by December 2005[7], via its European operation, AOL Europe, it still has about six million customers in the UK, France and Germany. Should Canadian healthcare software companies not take a cue from AOL, which in fact has also been re-branding, including changing its previous name, America Online? In other words, these companies might need to respond to developments in their markets of interest via a range structural, and other modifications or, in some cases, face possible extinction. In fact, as the case of AOL also shows, they might need to seek additional investments to improve their offerings, even consider mergers and acquisitions in other to remain competitive. In December 2005, online search engine Google confirmed its intention to invest $1bn for a 5% stake in AOL as part of a key strategic alliance, a deal which values AOL at $20bn, and would result in a global online advertising partnership that would make more of AOL's content available to users of Google[9]. The deal also effectively blocked software giant Microsoft rumored to be also interested in a deal with AOL, and confirms Google's determination to pay substantially in order to stop Microsoft gaining more-competitive edge in the profitable internet search sector. AOL and Google have been collaborating prior to now, the former, the latter's biggest client, responsible for about $429m, or 10%, of Google's revenue during the first nine months of 2005, for example. Incidentally, Yahoo was also gunning for a stake in AOL, but its talks with Time Warner collapsed in November 2005, purportedly, because the latter wanted to retain most stakes in AOL. By boosting its subscriber base, AOL would no doubt be enhancing its prospects for attracting advertisement dollars. Could Canadian software firms not adopt this model and apply it in the health sector, for example, offering a needed service free, acquiring a veritable subscriber base in the process, for which advertisers would be willing to pay? Here again, starting with this basic business idea, it would be necessary to do the sort of process cycle analysis mentioned earlier for the firm to determine the most appropriate service to offer in the particular market of interest. An example would be to develop a sophisticated search engine that would serve the need of either a mass or niche market, in the former case for examples, to help find the most current and comprehensive information on vitamins and minerals, in the latter, on orthopedic devices. On the other hand, the software firm might decide to offer seniors free, contextualized health information, developing software that are user-friendly, for example, visually, for this segment of the population. There might be already such products and services on the market, but how would the software firm know, and how could it plan to develop products/services that fill the quality gap, or improve on current offerings if it did not engage in the process analysis crucial to revealing such information? To use another Google example, the company has begun to alert its users about search results that could take them to malicious code, the Stop Badware Coalition data to flag sites probably hosting malicious software[10], a move Sun Microsystems and Lenovo, the leading Chinese computer manufacturer support. A search heading for such "poisoned" sites would be redirected to a warning page that says in bold type "Warning--the site you are about to visit may harm your computer!" In addition, it notes that users could "learn more about malware and how to protect yourself at StopBadware.org." It also says that users could return to the search page and choose a different result, try a different search, or continue to the risky site if they wished. According to Professor John Palfrey of Harvard Law School, and a protagonist of the idea, "We're not going to say don't do it...What we want to do is basically give people some more information about what might happen to their computer." Harvard is collaborating with Oxford University to offer labor support to the coalition's Web-monitoring initiative, with individuals reporting such sites, and volunteers checking before the flagging. According to Palfrey, it is a sort of "Neighborhood Watch" program, with sites not removed from search engines and the watch list available to other search engines. This example, no doubt also shows the potential for developing profitable software first identifying issues and problems that need resolution. As simplistic as it sounds, it is likely that there would many Canadian software firms, and in particular, that serve the health industry, which ignore this exercise, which no doubt explains at least partially, the narrow range of software products and services on the market in the country to start with, which likely mirrors that of those offered for exports. In other words, Canadian software firms should not restrict themselves to developing restricted products and services lines, for example, medical billing systems, but should be creative in meeting identified market needs. This does not mean that these firms could still not focus on niche or mass markets, the crucial thing being that they develop products for their chosen markets based on a thorough process cycle analysis of these markets. The health sector in particular offers immense opportunities for such innovative endeavors considering that everyone needs these products or services to a more or less extent in all countries. The problem is determining the software to each healthcare provider, jurisdiction, or country, or any other categorization of the intended markets that the software firm chose, needs revealed after a comprehensive process cycle analysis. There are ongoing grumblings in the net browser sector now because of Microsoft's decision to offer PC users its new browser as an integral component of an automatic update program, the update used to ensure users receive the latest patches for the browser's security loopholes. Internet Explorer 7 (IE7) is due later in the year (2006), although has been undergoing beta testing its completed version expected to be a "high priority" automatic download for Windows users, who would be "more secure and up-to-date," according to Microsoft. IE7 is the most profound update to the software in five years, with users of the completed software having the choices to install, install later, or not install at all, the browser not automatically making itself the default browser for those that chose to install it, although it would "transfer the user's previous homepage, favorites, search settings, and compatible toolbars." Microsoft is also developing software tools for big organizations to enable them block the driver's automatic download and installation. With competitors hot on its heels, literally, Microsoft is betting on this new browser to ward rivals such as Firefox, Netscape, and Opera, off, not surprising its market share of the Internet having dropped from 95% in June 2005 to 83.5% just a year later. This is another instance of the need to adopt the most appropriate business approach to the market. In other words, even after the process cycle analysis regarding market issues and problems that could reveal market needs and the product/service mix that could best meet them, Canadian software firms cannot overlook tactical issues such as the rollout approach of the product or service, or of licensing and other salient business issues.

The Wi-fi technologies we mentioned earlier offers a chance to illustrate again, the need for Canadian software firms, in particular operating in the health sector to reappraise their product/service mix on an ongoing basis based on the dictates of their process cycle analyses. In the U.K, proposals for rural areas to benefit from these technologies are under consideration[11]. Regulator Ofcom is planning to augment the power signals utilized in wi-fi networks and deliver broadband access to parts of the country lacking high-speed internet. Restrictions on the strength of wi-fi signals make it costly to implement the networks outside urban areas, but increasing signal power would reduce the cost of providing rural and remote areas with wireless networks drastically as this means fewer transmitters required. Signals in the U.S are ten times more powerful than in the U.K., now. The proposals on which Ofcom is currently consulting are boosting the power of wireless signals everywhere in the country, restricting the power increase to just rural areas, and a balance of both integrating a code of alliance to reduce signal interference. Hotspots are no doubt mushrooming in the U.K, but citywide seamless networks, termed mesh networks that enable individuals to roam freely from one hotspot to another with continuous internet access, are lacking, again the costs of deploying wireless transmitters to establish such meshed networks, in the way. Such networks are becoming commonplace in the U.S., and should they not in Canada? No doubt, there are reasons the demand is increasing in the U.S., for mesh networks, for example that the country allows more-potent wireless signals. Nonetheless, because these networks could also help speed up the diffusion of healthcare ICT, including of course healthcare software, opening up markets for software products in different domains of healthcare delivery, including to the rural and remote areas, the idea should interest Canadian software and other healthcare ICT firms. They should therefore seek ways to deploy these technologies within the country, and in fact, export their expertise abroad. This is an example of the sort of business model where technology offered free initially could create immense business opportunities that would wipe out the up-front investments costs, the cryptic market potential that Google, which is testing currently, a mesh network in Mountain View, California, that will be free to users, has perhaps already figured out. Indeed, according to Selina Lo, chief executive of home wi-fi antenna firm Ruckus which is collaborating with Google, "With lower power you have to use a lot more access points to form the network...A typical network will have hundreds or low thousands of access points. If you have power limits, these nodes have to be closer together and you need a lot more nodes." Lo, whose company, Ruckus, developed a wi-fi antenna for home users to hook up to city networks, also noted, "People running city networks know that the wi-fi in customers' home equipment is not powerful enough to do an outdoor long range connection. Our device is designed to bridge that connection." Here again is an example of an analysis of the market yielding an opening that Ruckus and

Google are now trying to fill. The potential for discovering such openings are simply immense in the health sector. Still on wi-fi opportunities, there are concerns in the U.K., for example, that boosting wi-fi signals' power in urban areas could result in interference between devices. This is another issue requiring resolution as indeed, "US hotspot operators are experiencing significant interference in this band," according to firms Ofcom consulted. Should Canadian software, Telco's, and other healthcare ICT firms not be contemplating solving this and other problems related to mesh networks, to fill the market demand that no doubt exists for such solutions at home and abroad? As earlier noted, opportunities abound in the health sector for Canadian software firms both within Canada and in the exports markets. One general approach to underscoring this, and it one that is truly general hence applicable to all countries, is to conceptualize healthcare delivery from a population health perspective, with the goal of healthcare delivery being primary, secondary, and tertiary disease prevention. Primary prevention means preventing diseases from occurring in the first place, secondary prevention, diagnosing them early and treating them promptly, and tertiary prevention treating them comprehensively to prevent and manage effectively their sequalae, including instituting the relevant rehabilitation measures. There is no health system in the world worth its salt that would not embrace this approach solely or in combination with others in the delivery of health services. Canadian software firms therefore only need to conduct the required process cycle analysis along these disease prevention lines for the particular overseas markets in which it is interested in order to reveal the underlying issues and processes relevant to the particular prevention level the firm chose to address, in the country. It would then be easier to determine the products and services, which the country's health systems and its peoples need. Besides disease prevention, health and wellness promotion also are increasingly important sources of healthcare software business as more and more peoples worldwide are starting to realize the benefits of staying healthy. There is no doubt about the potential market opportunities that exist for Canadian software companies in developing products and services for facilitating the accomplishment of these goals. In fact, there is also room for market segmentation in this domain, as indeed there are with others, for example, developing such products and services specifically for seniors, or for women, or children. Even within each general disease prevention category, not only could the issues involved with say health education differ between health systems in different countries, but they also could between health jurisdictions within the same country. In Canada, for example, telehealth would be a key technology in health services delivery in the territories, but they could also be crucial in provinces for service delivery to remote and rural locations, and in both instances, mesh networks could be valuable technologies to consider offering too. Some countries, particularly those in the developing world would certainly also need technologies for remote access to health services in many instances, but might likely lack the institutional, technical and other infrastructures to make the solutions that a Canadian software firm devised for a health region in Yukon for example, work for one in say, Lesotho. Nonetheless, the experience acquired implementing the technologies in the former could serve the firm well in working out an appropriate solution for the health region in the latter. In either case, however, the firm would need to conduct a thorough process cycle analysis in order to determine the issues and processes that need addressing and the appropriate software solutions to them. It is important to emphasize that these issues do not all have to health related. Simply put, any issue is relevant that in tandem with others result eventually in the outcome we term healthcare delivery. The other important aspect of the process cycle analysis is that we want to decompose the issues and reveal their underlying processes in an ongoing decomposition/exposition, or process cycle, in order to improve the outcome itself, of course improving along the way, certain key processes that result in this outcome. Thereafter, the aims of the software company and that of its client diverge, in a manner of speaking, the former to make money, the latter to achieve the dual healthcare delivery goals of delivering qualitative health services to the peoples while simultaneously curtailing health spending, and in this regard, whether the health system is privately or publicly funded is irrelevant. A curious point of convergence for these two though is that the former, in achieving its goal, needs to assist the latter in achieving its own, and vice versa, which further highlights the need for Canadian software firms to engage in the process cycle analysis mentioned above. This way, the firm would in a better position to justify the investments of its clients, and the clients, to achieve the dual healthcare delivery objectives.

The emphasis on population health, the soaring healthcare costs in many countries, population aging, the threat of bioterrorism, the continuing menace of HIV/AIDS, the devastation caused by earthquakes, Tsunamis, and hurricanes, among other natural disasters, the emergence of antibiotic resistance, and the potential imminent avian flu pandemic, are some of the health and related issues of contemporary significance. Some of these issues are of concern to some countries, and regions, others of global concern. These are all issues whose processes require software and healthcare ICT input at different levels and for different purposes. However, and as the list, which is by no means exhaustive shows, these issues are not all in strictly in the health domain. Indeed, some on the surface seem far removed form the health arena. Yet, they are potential sources of software business for Canadian software firms. There are opportunities for example to develop the necessary software for targeted, contextualized, health information provision services to which individuals could subscribe and receive up-to-date information on any health subject via a variety of multimedia portals. This could involve collaborating with other healthcare

ICT firms to deliver the content for example via computer games, mobile phones, or even the TV, the format of the content tailored to meet individual needs, for example, larger texts for the visually impaired and for seniors. Such services would not only save the subscriber the trouble of searching for this information themselves via traditional search engines, including the hassle of sifting the mass of information the engines return for the most relevant information, they would, the prospects of ending up on websites with inaccurate, stale, perhaps even biased information. There is no doubt that the market for this sort of service is potentially huge in many countries, in particular in those that have the technological backbone for implementing such a project. With the increasing need to rectify the information asymmetry from which the health industry, particularly the patients, has long suffered, particularly in these days of customer-focused health services delivery in many developed countries, the market for such services is only bound to increase. Thus, not only patients could benefit from such services, which the software company could couple with others, for example, personal health records services, healthcare professionals also need ready access to real-time, focused, and relevant information. The software firm could therefore in fact couple services for the latter with the service previously described, wherein, physicians and other healthcare professionals could have access to their patients' health information stored in the patients' personal health records (PHR), upon authorization. Such access could create communication avenues for consultation and treatment purposes. It could also facilitate information sharing by the patients' other healthcare service providers, say, chiropractor, or psychologist. In other words, these services should be in tandem with the push for the implementation of a comprehensive national health information system should proceed apace as it is in many countries. For example in the U.S, with the establishment of regional health information networks (RHIN), and in Canada, the integration of the essential elements of the electronic health records systems (EHR) that Canada Infoway oversees, must be other software programs that individuals could afford, and could all become integral parts of the national EHR systems. These issues of course will reveal, as is characteristic of the process cycle analysis, others, technical, for example, standards issues and those relating to the seamless integration of these disparate systems by different software firms, not to mention issues of security, the emergence of these issues as earlier noted should in fact inspire innovative novel software. Because networks are the basic elements of information sharing, some of the issues we mentioned earlier about wi-fi for example apply. There are of course going to be technical issues relating to mobile and wireless, increasingly used in health service delivery, and those for example, regarding enterprise or web-hosted applications, with the latter gaining increasing currency not just in business but also in the health industry, the latter especially with the ascendancy of the healthcare consumer in the healthcare delivery scheme. This example illustrates the potential benefits of a more organized process cycle analysis as issues reveal both opportunities and challenges, and the solutions to them all at once, as the process unfolds. It also reveals the potential for the distinctions we made earlier between vertical and horizontal markets for example to blur with such analysis, making it easier for software firms to be flexible in conceptualizing their business models, able for example to move seamlessly from either a licensing or service revenue base to a blend of both. With security software for example, the firm could develop products and services for corporate clients, for example hospitals and major healthcare providers, yet have products and services that the individual healthcare consumer could use, perhaps in relation to access to health information in a central database by both. Canadian software firms however, also need to be conversant with developments in the software industry in particular in the domain of interest to them, particular as it applies to the health industry for those interested in healthcare software. Radio Frequency ID (RFID) for example is one of the wireless devices increasingly applied in the health industry, although more used in for example, high-security projects such as the new digital passports and in smart cards. At the 2006, annual hacker gathering in Las Vegas on August 04, 2006, researchers demonstrated cloning (copying) with a laptop with an RFID reader, and a relatively cheap smart card writer, passports equipped with radio frequency identification (RFID) tags. They also noted that RFID tags embedded in such passports could identify U.S. passports from afar, making it possible for terrorists to use them as explosives trigger. While the researchers failed to reveal any flaws in the crypto protecting the integrity of the information stored in passports' chips, that is, they could not change the information even if they could copy it, reassuring considering the millions of Americans billed to receive their RFID passports, in October 2006, being able to copy such information is of concern enough. In fact, some European countries such as Germany have already issues such passports. With the possibility of being able to copy RFID-based corporate access cards, hence open, for example secure buildings, or vaults, for example a hospitals' blood bank, or pharmacy, should Canadian health software firms not consider focusing their attention on RFID security? Could a malicious person not copy another patients' RFID tag and impersonate the person perhaps in order to gain access to a secure location, or another person, for illegal purposes? Could tags on hospitals supplies not be tagging a replacement with the cloned tag of the original, again for malevolent purposes? It is clear therefore, that this technology, used increasingly in the health sector, needs to be more secure, including the prevention of data leakages, hence an area that Canadian software firms with an interest and expertise in developing security software could explore. The company's solution could apply to not just the corporate but also individual users of RFID. With regards passports for example, while the German government is seeking ways to solve the issues with the E-passports, for example, data leakages, with partially opened passports, some experts are suggesting a dual cover shield and an RFID tag specially made to prevent it being readable until one opens the passports fully. Others carry their passports in an aluminum pouch, or other such protective devices. To give another example, this time, involving software firms focusing on some issues and not others, Hewlett-Packard (HP) August 04, 2006, announced the renewal of its agreement to provide services to the Canadian Imperial Bank of Commerce (CIBC) until 2013, an extra four years to the original contract. This involves HP overseeing the enterprise infrastructure of bank's electronic banking services such as ATM, Internet banking, point-of-sale transactions, wire payment, and fraud detection. However, the deal, worth $1.2 billion over the next seven years, also involves HP maintaining the bank's network and storage management systems, applications and operating systems, but not its desktop support technologies, which the bank itself would handle. Thus, as with these examples, one of the key challenges Canadian health software firms would increasingly confront is the business model to adopt in the global exports markets, and indeed, even in markets at home. One of the key concerns about business model is not adopting one that would be inflexible, but that is not to say, as the above examples show, that software firms could not focus on some products and services to the exclusion of others. It all depends on the firm's strategic objectives, its core competencies, its markets of interests, and a host of other factors.

In seeking opportunities in exports markets, Canadian health software firms must not forget those that abound in the North American markets, particularly in the U.S., which traditionally, remains Canada's major trading partner. The firms therefore also need to track goings-on in the software industry in the U.S. in general, and in its health sector in particular. Not only could engaging in process cycle analysis for the U.S market likely yield avenues for businesses hitherto unknown, developments in that country could indeed, create incentives for innovative software products and services for markets not just in that country, but which Canadian software firms could market back home, and elsewhere. For example, members of the Federal Communications Commission in the U.S. at their monthly meeting on August 03, 2006 again set in motion their quest for a wider rollout of what some termed a viable "third pipe" for the many areas with limitations in broadband choices to DSL or cable modems. There is no doubt that if successful, and broadband over power lines (BPL) takes off in earnest, more Americans, especially in rural and remote areas, would be able to hook up to high-speed Internet access. Could Canadian healthcare software firms not exploit the market opportunities that this development could open up? This development in effect also means that markets, in which cable and DSL (digital subscriber line) currently hold sway, would have little choice but to lower consumers' bills[12]. What does this imply for widening the market scope of software companies, particularly in the health sector in terms of health content delivery for example? The FCC adopted an order to consolidate efforts on the first set of rules it issued for the technology in 2004, for example the so-called Bell companies, no longer have to lease new fiber installations to competitors at all, but that they must share any existing copper connections to homes/offices once upgraded to fiber optics. Some inside and outside the industry had complained that these rules merely reinforced the monopoly of the telephone (Bell) companies such as Verizon Communications, Qwest Communications and BellSouth, which they claimed FCC shielded from competition for the residential and small businesses markets. With regulators, easing concerns over the burgeoning Internet service resulting in damaging interference with radio signals reliant on nearby frequencies, such as those typically used in aviation, which the initial regulations aimed to prevent, as FCC Chairman Kevin Martin noted at the meeting mentioned earlier, "It is my hope that our rules will allow BPL systems to flourish." Canadian healthcare software firms should also note, regarding these latest regulations that the Commission refused requests the amateur radio community, TV broadcasters and the aeronautical industry to exclude or prohibit BPL offerings at certain frequencies, citing lack of sufficient evidence of interference to warrant the extra limitations. The issue of such frequencies interference has indeed plagued the health sector for sometime now, not just in the U.S but also in Canada and elsewhere, an issue that has no doubt hindered healthcare ICT diffusion in these countries one way or another. Considering the restrictions on the use of mobile phones in hospitals for similar reasons, for example, and the increasing efforts to make the Internet more widely available on mobile phones and more user-friendly, too, what would be the implications of these new regulations on the increasing applications of mobile and wireless technologies in the health sector in the U.S? Could Canadian software firms not benefit from the immense market opportunities that these regulations might create potentially increasing wireless local area networks (WLAN) access points and enhancing integration with health facilities' wired LANs for example? Given the increasing demand by healthcare providers in real-time access to current and accurate patient data and information, such as case and medications histories, lab results, and even health insurance information at the point of care (POC), are the markets for a variety of software products and services not potentially huge, and should Canadian firms not partake in them? This of course is not to say that WLANs and their end units would still not have to comply with the Institute of Electrical and Electronics Engineers (IEEE) 802.11 (and the later upgrades) standards for safe wireless transmission in health facilities. Nonetheless, could developing the required software for the variety of healthcare delivery tasks that mobile and wireless technologies could enable, and enhance not be potential major revenue sources for these firms, while they would helping healthcare providers and indeed, the entire health system achieve the dual healthcare delivery objectives of providing qualitative health services cost-effectively and efficiently? Despite that the quest for ferrying Internet access over the electrical grid started many years ago, the U.S. has just about fifty such systems even now, most in fact still in the developmental or experimental phase, in the main due to resistance from amateur radio operators who insisted that BPL unfettered could interrupt their systems. However, commercial interest in the technology is waxing stronger with two firms in 2005 announcing their intention to offer BPL to 2 million homes and businesses in the north of Texas, for example, soon. California regulators in spring 2006 also gave testing the technology and service in the state the nod and investors are lining up to fund products and services to get things going. Should Canadian software firms not participate in this potentially lucrative exports market? Does this example not also underscore the need for Canadian healthcare software firms to engage in the sort of process cycle analysis mentioned earlier for their markets and products/services of interests? To underscore further the growing commercial interests in these technologies, BPL provider Current Communications Group, already operating in Cincinnati, recently obtained over $200 million in financial support from key corporate players for examples, EarthLink, Google, and General Electric. Does this not suggest the immense potential of these markets and that of these technologies on ubiquitous broadband deployment in the U.S and in other countries too? Considering the major role that amateur radio operators played in the aftermath of Hurricane Katrina in facilitating communication between relief agencies and other services though, the FCC is not likely to ignore every of the group's complaints regarding interference. This again, is another example of the reason the process cycle analysis we have harped on so much in our discussion to be an ongoing exercise for Canadian healthcare software firms, including tracking developments on these issues also in Canada, and in countries to which they plan to exports their products and services.

$\mathbf{A}$s we noted earlier, the mobile and wireless technologies markets is going to

be a major growth market for the healthcare software industry in the near future. In fact, there is already a great deal of interest in these technologies as they offer real-time access and mobility, two important elements of the paradigm shift in healthcare delivery that developments in both the developed and developing countries are in a sense coalescing to promote, namely population health. This is not to mention the variety of multimedia features they could offer including mobile TV, all veritable health content delivery portals. In most countries, increasing healthcare costs are driving the push to reduce hospitalization stays and medications expenses, for examples, and to encourage ambulatory and domiciliary treatment of patients. In many others, particularly in the developed world, population aging, and the increasing prevalence of chronic health problems are additional drivers of these management approaches and in particular of disease prevention as many chronic diseases could. In developing countries, whereas, where demographics and disease patterns are different, most being young populations, communicable diseases, are their major health issue, the drivers for primary prevention, in particular, and for secondary and tertiary prevention as well, for which remote access to health services is key, considering the dearth of healthcare facilities and professionals and of technical infrastructures. In both developed and developing countries therefore, the need for prevention at all levels, and of course, to delivery qualitative health services cost-effectively and efficiently, is rife. There is no doubt that healthcare software and ICT of various sorts have key roles to play in the actualization of these goals, and that Canadian software firms only need to, again, carry out the necessary process cycle analysis for its intended markets I n order to determine the right product/service mix to offer. Palm Pilots and BlackBerrys are already part of many doctors gadgets arsenal. These devices are packed-filled with a variety of software to enhance productivity, for example, to facilitate access health information, and communication with patients and colleagues. Canadian software companies could explore these features, add to, and improve upon them. For example, mobile and wireless technologies, including Bluetooth are confronting increasingly threats of viruses and other malicious logic. As with other applications in the health sector, keeping patient health information and other health data secure is a major ongoing issue that threatens the use of health information and communication technologies. With hackers increasingly targeting health institutions, the markets for solutions to software security are indeed, enormous in many countries. Canadian software companies would also find sizeable markets in most countries developing software for mobile and wireless markets for the use of these technologies in healthcare settings for examples operating theaters, imaging centers, and labs, and others where they are best suited due to known difficulties installing network cabling in these settings. In other words, some of these firms might want to focus on these niche markets, others, on the other hand, on more mass-type markets for examples, markets for hand-held devices that every healthcare professional, and indeed, client, could use, mentioned earlier. They could indeed, focus on any other medical mobile and wireless technologies for examples, for patient monitoring, treatment and medical management, consultation, lab result reporting, robotic delivery carts, mobile workstations for nurses and doctors, and real-time health insurance eligibility verification and claims processing. These technologies would are also increasingly deployed in niche healthcare markets for logging inventory on wireless devices, which would improve resource management, the potential for inventory tracking ensuring the seamless flow of medical supplies and equipments thereby facilitating supply chain management. Wireless technologies would also increasingly aid patient management by paramedics en-route to hospital in the ambulance, real-time patient data, vital signs, and on-the-spot investigations for examples blood sugar, and EKGs transmitted to the ER in various multimedia formats, paramedics able to receive emergency management tips from ER and other doctors awaiting patient at the hospital before the ambulance gets there. These measures could no doubt save many lives, helping to reduce both health and economic burden of diseases, the markets for Canadian software firms for innovative product and service offerings in this market no doubt remarkable in many countries. Hand-held scanning devices are also niche-market type wireless technologies, and would be increasingly in use by healthcare professionals for example, nurses to gain access to Internet-based databases of medication records, ensuring by scanning patients' bar-coded bracelet and medication that they are receiving the correct medication and dose, and when they should, thereby preventing medical errors and saving lives. Pharmacists would also increasingly use wireless technologies as hand-held devices to access patients' drug profiles, calculate dosing, and order refills, and doctors would be able to management their patients remotely using these devices, for example to alert them to take medications, to monitor their progress, in and outside hospital, including detecting critical situations that require hospitalization before they occur. The deployment of wireless technologies would increasingly gain currency particularly with the emphasis on ambulatory and domiciliary care mentioned earlier, wireless devices used increasingly as stand-alone or as telemetry monitors, able to track patients' vital signs, ECK, blood sugar, and blood pressure and transmit the values to a central nursing workstation. These devices, for whose use the training patients is relatively easy, would no doubt facilitate the management of chronic diseases that are prevalent in many developed countries, hence the potential for their markets to grow in the near future immense, more so as the population ages in these countries, increasing the prevalence of these conditions even more. As noted earlier, primary prevention is also an integral aspect of the management of these conditions that would benefit from the use of wireless technologies, for example, in health education campaigns and health information provision for health promotion in general. Canadian software firms need therefore to once again, conduct process cycle analyses for the issues involved in the use of these technologies, in general or in specific markets, one, security, we mentioned earlier, and others, for example, the slow speed of WLAN compared to LAN transmission, would certainly emerge, the results of these analyses, the starting points for strategic intent. Indeed, the conceptualizing of software and ICT in general as an enabler is gradually changing and in the health industry in particular, these technologies need to be able to do more than enable. Software is increasingly conceptualized as constitutive, sort of "embedded" in the entire system, and akin to its organic constituents, is involved actively in tandem with the other constituents in the system's evolution. For example, healthcare professionals need accurate and current information on their patients, in real-time. As we have noted thus far, Canadian software firms following a thorough process cycle analysis could determine the crucial underlying issues and processes involved in this need, and the most appropriate software to facilitate its realization. However, this is not enough for the maximization of the potential of these technologies to result in the best fit so to say regarding their ability to increase the chances of realizing the dual healthcare delivery objectives of qualitative healthcare delivery, cost-effectively and efficiently. In other words, Canadian software firms might be not measure up to their competitors that in keeping with this concept of software being potentially constitutive, took their products a step further, for example, to bridge the chasm between information need and decision-making. This added benefit of the software would likely give their competitors an edge in the market, which again underlines the need for a comprehensive understanding of the status in the market, even after determining potentially marketable products and services, in order to garner competitive advantage. The software market is increasingly client-focused, in both generic and specific terms. Software companies need to meet client needs, and perhaps surpass client expectations as the above example shows, and to recognize the need for their clients to meet and may surpass theirs, the latter, the reason another increasingly lucrative software market in the health industry is for customer relations management applications and services. The trend toward IP hosted contact center applications is in no doubt, its improved features such as simplified and speedy start-up cycles, and remote management and agent competencies driving growth in the contact center markets. With developments in other business models occasioned by cost containment and revenue, both as earlier noted, of increasing importance to health systems worldwide, for example, outsourcing and off shoring, and self-service, also nascent, all predicated on progress in and influence of voice-over IP (VoIP) technologies and standards-based software overriding proprietary, hardware-based solutions, profound market changes are indeed, imminent. Canadian software firms with interests in these business models no doubt have significant opportunities for enhanced and perhaps customized product/service value propositions in healthcare markets at home and abroad.

Today's health systems, as noted earlier are also under pressure to justify their investments, including in software and other healthcare ICT, and to optimize resources in general, all in the attempt to reduce the spending of funds that are increasingly difficult for them to find anyway. There are also other business drivers in countries such as the U.S., for example, the need to comply with regulations such as the Health Insurance Portability and Accountability Act (HIPAA) and Sarbanes-Oxley Act, to ensure their survival, literally, make hosted contact center solutions' mix of rapid implementation, negligible upfront costs, favorable revenue stream/expense balance, labor free-up, pluses. The newer models of contact center services would make it much easier for Canadian software and ICT firms to compete on the global stage with competitors in countries such as India with erstwhile labor-costs advantage. This is more so as other countries, particularly in Asia, such as Vietnam, and the Philippines, which also have a large English-speaking, and perhaps even less expensive expertise base, are entering the markets. While it might seem on the surface that countries such as Canada could not compete with these countries on labor costs-basis, however, with the increasing broadband and VoIP penetration in Canada, a novel business model for this market, at-home/remote agents, would probably level the playing field to a certain extent. This model, poised to become the industry standard, utilizes remote and at-home agents reducing seat costs, fostering higher agent retention rates and increasing the chances of recruiting more and better qualified agents, all likely to reduce operating costs, and to enhance the prospects of profitability of call center firms. For Canadian firms, these benefits would likely also increase their chances of competing successfully in international markets, particularly coupling their contact center with speech recognition services. The increasing trend of Western-based enterprises that utilize call centers in Asian countries to look further West due to a number of developments in some of the Asian markets including fraud, and language barriers, would also likely work in Canadian software firms' favor. These firms however, need to follow closely the evolution of customer relations management in the health sector, as different business models evolve, and this important function of the enterprise becomes even more so with the shift in healthcare delivery paradigm mentioned earlier. They would also need to determine the outsourcing model that most suits their competencies and the markets of interest, for example, completely taking over the IT departments of healthcare institutions or providing measured expertise to in-house staff in an agreed working alliance. Many healthcare organizations in developed countries such as the U.S are already outsourcing radio-diagnostic services to overseas radiologists for example, in India. The markets for such services are massive, and the technologies involved offer immense market potential in both the countries involved. Again, this highlights the need for Canadian software firms to be familiar with developments clinical, administrative, business, and otherwise in the health sector, particularly in their markets of interests. Indeed, Canadian healthcare software firms need to be current regarding developments in different domains of their endeavors for example, in the business and technological domains. Healthcare organizations for example are paying more attention to licensing management. Indeed, many are no longer relying on an in-house software licensing solution, which could in no time, become outdated and ineffectual with changes, which are often inevitable in both the healthcare organization, and the industry, hence instead moving toward utilizing third-party solutions. No doubt building and maintaining proprietary software could be cheaper, as would be training, and integration costs. However, even healthcare organizations have to deal with change, for example, increasing and unanticipated levels of unlicensed usage, hacker threats, new products, and service developments mandating changes to legacy systems, the rapid growth of and increasing use of CRM systems mentioned earlier, and enterprise resource planning systems (ERP) in health services, both necessitating changes in the operations of the organization, including in software license management, which could be difficult with an in-house system as it often outdated failing to keep pace with the ensuing rapid systems changes in organization's business units. The customized solutions built in-house often are not flexible or open-ended enough to cope with healthcare organizations' changing technical and business imperatives. Licenses, linked as they are with the products they protect must flow seamlessly with these products for their entire lifecycle. Hence, license management system need be able to communicate with dissimilar databases, and receive input from numerous back-office systems, among other important tasks. These are tasks in which in-house systems, typically customized for a current need, rather than to be able to integrate with systems perhaps not even acquired by the healthcare organization, are inherently deficient. For these and other reasons, including deficient expertise in building a scalable and flexible in-house license management system by IT personnel in healthcare organizations, many would rather outsource this task to third party software firms, a no doubt, huge market both in Canada and overseas. As Canadian software firms become more export-oriented, some would find themselves seeking business opportunities or investing in countries with weak governance, where governments are not willing or are unable to take up their responsibilities, hence these firms exposed to a variety of risks ethical dilemmas. Some of these issues include compliance with the law and with international regulations in a milieu of chaos or under unfavorable conditions, increased attention to managing investments, dealing with known and trusted business partners and clients, and with public sector officials, and getting involved with local issues and speaking out against crime and misconduct. Government ineptness in these weak zones in which roughly 15% of the world's population live, mostly in sub-Saharan Africa, result in wide-ranging defects in political, economic and civic institutions that, in turn, result in corruption, violence, crime, in effect, compromising economic growth and social development. Canadian software firms with interests in these zones, which incidentally have huge and largely untapped markets, need to be aware of the challenges such environments pose and be ready to confront and overcome these challenges. The business opportunities for Canadian healthcare software are indeed, legion, both within Canada and on the world stage. With the increasing market competition either way, these firms need to become more agile in order to survive, let alone thrive. Part of this agility would entail a commitment to appreciating fully the issues individually and severally germane to their industry and markets, both now, and in the future. This would require as we have argued all through thus far, engaging in the process cycle analysis relevant to the domain for which they seek fuller understanding. This seemingly endless multiplicity of efforts is an essential ingredient for doing business not just in the health industry but also at all in our contemporary hypercompetitive business climate. As we also noted earlier noted, with opportunities necessarily come challenges, which process cycle analysis would also reveal, and which in fact, are the inevitable other side of the ongoing quality improvement that these firms and their clients not only need but to which, following on the certainty of change, they must each adhere lest become moribund.

References

1. Available at:

http://newsvote.bbc.co.uk/mpapps/pagetools/print/news.bbc.co.uk/2/hi/technology/5238992.stm Accessed on August 02, 2006

2. Available at: http://www.netidme.com/netidme.asp Accessed on August 03, 2006

3. Available at: http://www.statcan.ca/Daily/English/060126/d060126b.htm, August 05, 2006

4. Available at: http://www.statcan.ca/Daily/English/060731/d060731a.htm Accessed on August 5, 2006

5. Available at: http://www.statcan.ca/english/Subjects/Labour/LFS/lfs-en.htm

Accessed on August 05, 2006

6. Beckstead, D., M. Brown, G. Gellatly and C. Seaborn. 2003. *A Decade of Growth: The Emerging Geography of New Economy Industries in the 1990s*. The Canadian Economy in Transition Research Paper Series 11-622-MIE No. 003. Analytical Studies Branch. Ottawa: Statistics Canada.

7. Available at:

http://www.medicalnewstoday.com/medicalnews.php?newsid=48842&nfid=al Accessed on August 5, 2006

8. Available at:

http://newsvote.bbc.co.uk/mpapps/pagetools/print/news.bbc.co.uk/2/hi/business/5238346.stm

Accessed on August 5, 2006

9. Available at: http://news.bbc.co.uk/go/pr/fr/-/2/hi/business/4547672.stm
Accessed on August 5, 2006

10. Available at http://news.com.com/2102-7349_3-
6102529.html?tag=st.util.print
Accessed on August 5, 2006

11. Available at: http://news.bbc.co.uk/go/pr/fr/-
/2/hi/technology/5230460.stm
Accessed on August 5, 2006

12. Available at: http://news.com.com/2102-1028_3-
6101925.html?tag=st.util.print
Accessed on August 7, 2006

The Future of the Healthcare Software Business in Canada

Software business in Canada's health sector is evolving, but not fast enough,

for reason attributable to both the software and health industries. The health industry is information-intensive, yet lags considerably behind other such industries in its use of healthcare information and communication technologies, the reasons legion. Software firms have also to exploit the opportunities that the health sector offers for innovative product and service development to any remarkable extent. Meanwhile, the expectations of the healthcare consumer for health services delivery continue to increase and to be more sophisticated, and the software industry continues to miss significant sources of revenue generation. With the increasing emphasis on consumer-driven health services provision, we could expect these expectations to become even more complex and suave. Incidentally, meeting the expectations of Canadians of their cherished Medicare is imperative not just for their sake. Indeed, the country's health system has to find the means to continue to deliver the high quality healthcare that its peoples have come to expect of it, only this time with a keener eye on its budget. It is no secret that the country's health spending is on the rise, billed at $142 billion in 2005, the most chunk of the country's gross domestic product (GDP,) 10.4 cents for every dollar in the economy, noted the Canadian Institute for Health Information (CIHI[1],) a 5% increase, post adjustment for inflation, from the $131.8 billion of 2004. CIHI also estimated the country's total drug expenditure to be $24.8 billion in 2005, an 11% rise over 2004, its estimates for total drug expenditure per person in Canada for 2005, $770, a 10.2% increase over

2004[2]. In fact, healthcare spending continues to rise as a percentage of the GDP, from 7% for example, in 1975, to 10% by 1992, and following a brief fall, rose to 10.2% in 2004. In fact, both the private and public parts of health expenditure are increasing faster than are inflation and the country's economy. A new study that the Vancouver-based, Fraser Institute released on October 31, 2005 showed that Medicare would consume over 50% of total revenues from all sources in seven of 10 provinces in the country by 2022[3]. Is this sustainable, and should the country not be seeking ways to reduce this spending and in fact, of improving rather than compromising healthcare delivery simultaneously? Canada spends about $4,411 per person on health, as high as $4,820 in Alberta and low as $3,878 in Quebec. The country is fourth highest per capita health spender among the Organization for Economic Cooperation and Development (OECD) countries, after the United States ($5,635 Cdn), Norway ($3,807) and Switzerland ($3,781)[1]. Healthcare spending as a percentage of the GDP continues to soar, according to CIHI, the growth in private health spending slightly outpacing that in public spending for 2005. As earlier noted, medications costs account for a significant portion of Canada's health spending, for which individuals and employers mostly pay. After hospitalization costs, drug costs come next as the fastest-growing category of health spending, the latter billed to gulp about 18% of total health expenditures in 2005. Is it any wonder that the expectations of Canadians of health services would likely continue to increase and become more sophisticated considering that they are paying a significant portion of these medications costs? Should we not expect them to put increasing pressure on the health system to reduce these costs? Should the health system itself not intrinsically want to reduce these and other costs soaring health spending, which if not curtailed could potentially compromise the ability of governments both at federal and provincial/territorial levels to conduct their affairs and to deliver other important services to their peoples? Would ever-increasing health spending not in fact have a negative effect on the country's goal of sustainable economic growth and development? Would meeting, the expectations of Canadians regarding health service delivery not improve their health overall and reduce health spending, and is therefore not imperative for the country to achieve? What are the implications of these issues for the country's software industry, and indeed, its healthcare ICT industry in general? Could a negative cycle of events develop with woes of the country's health system feeding into other aspects of its economy and what could this portend for the country's health system, its economy, and indeed, its future? These are pertinent questions on profound issues. Yet, this adverse cycle is not bound to happen, although neither could, we simply make it disappear by fiat. We need to do something concrete to prevent it. In other words, not only the health and software industries are at risk, not meeting the increasingly urbane healthcare consumer expectations in Canada, the whole economy is. To be sure, the increased drug spending in the country is not totally, unexpected considering the increasing aging of the country's population, seniors being the most prolific users of the health system, many with more than one chronic disease, warranting the use of several medications. However, drugs are also becoming more expensive. In any case, many of these chronic diseases are preventable, and it is possible to delay the onset and slow the progression of others, aspects of these diseases, prevention, short and long-term management, and all, in which healthcare software and healthcare ICT in general have key roles, mostly unexplored by Canadian healthcare software firms. As earlier noted, the health industry is rich in content, which besides communicating and sharing it needs to store, and manage effectively. Besides software involved in treatment purposes, the need of the health industry for software for enterprise content management (ECM) for example, which the Association for Information and Image Management (AIIM) in 2005 defined as the technologies used to capture, manage, store, preserve, and deliver content and documents related to organizational processes, is also obvious. There is no doubt that many healthcare institutions in Canada still practice paper-based records management and document management, for which they would need ECM, whose new definition embraces these legacy systems. It also covers other issues concerning, again, what many of these health institutions should be trying to do nowadays, that is, upgrading their filing and retrieval systems converting their content from paper to digital, and improving their digital systems with cutting-edge technologies to improve further, the efficiency and effectiveness of their operations overall. There is thus, no doubt, about the immense market opportunities for healthcare software firms to market ECM, which could also help these institutions and other healthcare providers improve their business processes, via improving their record and auditing management, information and knowledge communication and sharing, and content standardization, among others. ECM could help these clients turn unstructured content for examples text documents, audio and video files, email, XML, transactional data, pictures, and images, via an automatic learning process into richer and more valuable content. In other words, the health sector offers Canadian software firms immense opportunities for creativity, for example, in developing ECM software that would not just enable functions, but that would be "constitutive", becoming an integral part of the evolution of the processes involved in the functions in question, materializing. Such constitutive ECM, for example would be able to learn and acquire new filtering, search, and routing pathways, semantic networks and approaches to organizational classification, facilitating better retention-rule decision making, able to choose records to discard, or to archive. It would be able to take such decisions regarding for examples, text messaging and emails, which being more used in the health services these days, could clog up the system quickly, otherwise. Many healthcare institutions and providers want to migrate from their piecemeal electronic document management systems (EDMS), which some have had for more than two decades, aiming to capitalize on the scalability and costs savings of ECM offering the functionalities seamlessly of these individual workflow, imaging, COLD/ERM, and document management systems, the typical functional aspects of the EDMS of yore. Many healthcare organizations are also seeking to address a variety of business and applications needs and would no doubt embrace technologies that could facilitate such tasks as forms processing, insurance claims processing, editorial and multi-channel publishing, engineering documentation, new drugs applications, and the distribution and archiving of monthly, quarterly, or annual financial reports, among others. Besides the need to save time, increase efficiency and indeed save money, which versioning, reformatting and ownership issues could compromise, and which ECM software could enhance, ECM also helps with compliance issues, for example, as mandated in law in Canada, with the need to securely store and retrieve an array of health information and other content for a stipulated period. Furthermore, by facilitating information sharing, it enhances one of the main clinical benefits of the deployment of healthcare software and indeed, other healthcare ICT, thus by extension, the ability of the Canadian health system to achieve the dual objectives of qualitative health services provision while simultaneously reducing health spending. Is it any wonder then that IBM has decided to acquire FileNet Corp., which assists firms route data via business applications in a $1.6 billion deal the company announced on August10, 2006? IBM's software division, which reportedly makes the most profit for the company, has had 38 acquisitions since 2001 as IBM pursues its "information on demand" value proposition to its clients, FileNet Corp., the company's second sizable software purchase in one week. The company on Aug. 3 2006 acquired for $740 million, MRO Software Inc., which develops asset-tracking software. FileNet is a major player in the enterprise content management (ECM) market, which IBM plans to grow over 10% annually over the next five years, even with major firms such as EMC Corp., and Oracle Corp., in contention[3]. Would IBM's Canada operations be foraying into the enterprise content management market in the health sector with its latest acquisition? Are Canadian software firms in general not interested in exploring this wide-open and massive market? Does the fact that IBM sold its PC business to China's Lenovo in 2005, and its software business, which incidentally it shunned 25 years ago, for the tangible hardware business, effectively sanctioning the emergence of Intel and Microsoft, not say something for potential of the software business? Could IBM's "on-demand" business model not have much to benefit from exploring the healthcare markets?

We cannot overemphasize the point about Canadian software firms exploring Canada's huge and in the main virgin healthcare markets, and "exploring" is the keyword here. These firms need to go out and explore the markets. They need to offer the health industry innovative products and services that meet the needs of the healthcare consumer and other industry stakeholders. They need to foray vertically or horizontally into the markets, or in fact, both ways. As we noted earlier, the laid-back attitude of the health industry toward healthcare software and ICT in general is legendary, and this is not only in Canada, but also in many other countries, developed and developing alike. The reasons for this attitude are variegated, rooted for example, in entrenched health industry customs, costs of the technologies, technophobia, fear of loss of status, litigation, and productivity, among others, understanding the interplay of which is mandatory for software firms to navigate the health industry, successfully. In other words, one of the first things a Canadian software firm needs to do in order to exploit the healthcare market opportunities maximally is to engage identify the issues that the health industry confronts, and that are lurking, health related, or concerning a variety of other issues in non-health domains, for example, technical, regulatory, legal, and even cultural domains. They not only need to identify these issues, they need to decompose them, and reveal their underlying issues and processes, decomposing and exposing further, in a perpetual process cycle analysis, hence able to determine the appropriate software required to facilitate, or modify somehow, these issues and their processes. These modifications, which would be what the market needs, would therefore, be what the software firms would offer it. This exercise does not only benefit the software firms. It also does, the healthcare consumer, and indeed, the entire health system. By developing software for example, that could give doctors and other healthcare providers the confidence to eschew defensive practice, would the software firm not have a guaranteed market among these healthcare providers, would such software not save the healthcare consumer needless lab and other investigations and medications, and the health system money, may be even substantially? Would the software firm, not be contributing to the health and economic progress of the country, simultaneously making money, too? Considering the possible domains impinging on health service delivery from within and without the health sector, are the possibilities for creativity by software firms not in fact limitless? This is even more so that no health system is ever going to be perfect, and that there would always be new issues with which to contend, an imminent outbreak of a previously-unknown virus, for example, or new medical knowledge that warrant changes to established procedures, which would require not just upgrading, but in fact, perhaps replacing legacy systems. However, how could a software firm be current with these developments if not involved in an ongoing process cycle analysis of its market segments of interest? It is not likely that all software firms would have the resources, capabilities, or competencies to carry out such exercises, and should outsource it to the professionals and firms that do, if they did not. There is no doubt that the benefits that would accrue from so doing would far outweigh the costs in the long and even short-terms. Would it not be important for Canadian software firms to know for example that according to a report by the Canadian Medical Association and Canada Health Infoway, released in summer 2006, up to 76% of Canadian physician offices have a personal computer, and 64% of those computers have high-speed Internet access, 57%, connected to an office computer network[4]? Would it also not matter to them that the report also indicated that the time and effort required in deploying, an electronic medical record (EMR) and its start-up costs were the chief obstacles to its adoption? Would these not be issues for decomposing, in order to finding solutions to them, for example, offering scalable, incremental EMR technologies at affordable prices, with reduced learning curves? Would Canadian software firms not also find it useful for developing strategic objectives knowing what physicians who use healthcare ICT do with them? The report, for example, also showed that Canadian physicians that utilize healthcare ICT in their practices do so most often to seek evidence-based drug information, 54%; to perform electronic continuing medical education, 48%; to book patient appointments, 47%; to e-mail colleagues for clinical reasons, 46% and; 36% use these technologies to receive lab or other test results[5]. Could this information not help software firms determine the areas of physicians' activities for which to consider developing software? Canadian software firms indeed, need to seek and utilize such valuable information in their product and service development efforts, as doing otherwise would likely increasingly compromise a firm's competitiveness as, which we also earlier noted, the average Canadian healthcare consumer becomes more discerning in its expectations of service quality and costs. In other words, why would such a consumer patronize a healthcare provider, for example, an optometrist, whose services cost more, rather than another, who provides the same services, perhaps even at higher quality due to its use of certain healthcare software, less expensively? Would the software firm able to develop software for optometrists, based on a thorough process cycle analysis of the issues and processes that culminate in the services that they deliver, not only have a competitive edge in the market, but in fact generate more revenues than one that ignored this exercise and has no appropriate product or service to offer? Would the healthcare provider also not acquire and retain more clientele than its competition? Would both not have been meeting the expectations of the healthcare consumer for those services, thereby, preventing the prevalence of say, glaucoma, with perhaps significant savings in disease burden, in human and material terms? With the increasing tendency toward private sector participation in the country's health systems, healthcare consumers are in fact likely to be even shrewder, and competing healthcare providers more inclined to adopt healthcare software and health information and communication technologies in general, in order to remain competitive, perhaps even survive. In this regard, it would also no doubt the valuable for Canadian healthcare software firms to know that whereas Canada's general practitioners are increasingly embracing healthcare ICT, a multi-country study of the computerization of primary care in the country revealed that it lags behind most other industrialized countries. The study, "Adoption of IT by GP/FMs: A 10-Country Comparison," is an international review that Dr. Denis Protti (PhD), a professor in the University of Victoria's School of Health Information Science, conducted and which Canada Health Infoway and the Canadian Medical Association (CMA) jointly released in mid-July, 2006[6]. According to the study, about 90% of physician offices in nine of the 10 foreign countries examined have computers used for clinical functions, versus about 20%, in Canada. The countries studied are England, Scotland, Denmark, Sweden, Norway, the Netherlands, Austria, Germany, New Zealand and Australia, and Canada, e-prescribing quite common in these other countries. As Dr. Protti noted, that these countries differ in many ways including regarding population demographics, health system organization and funding, for examples, most GPs, as they are in Canada, are private practitioners paid fee-for-service. He also noted some factors important in ICT diffusion among GPs in these countries, among others, government financial support; the utilization of "pay for performance" inducements that inspired doctors to automate their offices; support by medical association and licensing bodies; and governments and medical bodies' certification of health software and ICT vendors. The buy-in by lead GPs is also important, and according to Dr. Protti, "The good news for Canada, is that the factors identified in other countries as supporting the implementation and adoption of information technology for clinical purposes are present in at least some provinces," but should in fact be, in all provinces and territories. This perhaps explains the observation by Richard Alvarez, Infoway's president and chief executive officer that Canada must intensify its efforts to draw level, at least, with its global peers, noting, "We need to stop running a 21st-century health system using 19th-century paperwork." Dr. Ruth Collins-Nakai, president of the Canadian Medical Association, also noted, "The most fundamental and important message (in the report) is that physicians themselves must be involved in evaluating, selecting and implementing the types of electronic systems they will be expected to use in clinical care." This underscores the need for healthcare software firms to engage in the process cycle analysis mentioned above, which would necessarily involve understanding and appreciating the needs of those healthcare providers included, who would use the software and ICT technologies proposed. It is also important to involve the systems' end-user from the start and at all stages of project implementation to facilitate the realization of the all-important buy-in mentioned above. Among the eleven countries studied, in Australia, 87% of practices are computerized, 67.5% with e-mail capabilities, 63% using online tools to order and receive pathology tests, and 49% of practices utilizing electronic referral systems. In Austria on the other hand, 34% of doctors are on contract providing health services, publicly funded, all linked to a national social security database of which health information is a part, 75% of private sector GPs with automated physician offices. Over 97% of GPs in England have automated offices, mostly used in e-prescribing, about 30% of offices essentially paperless. In Denmark, over 90% of GP offices utilize electronic medical records (EMRs), computers used for tasks such as discharge summaries, and for the management of lab requests/results, prescriptions, and appointments, and for bills processing. Forty percent of

German GPs use computers, almost all in Norway, where about all also use EMRs, and digital records are legal. Ninety seven percent of GPs in the Netherlands use health information systems, with 94% using them for medical notes, and over 90% of medications, e-prescribed. Almost all GPs in Scotland use EMRs, and over 90%, computers routinely in their offices, in New Zealand, 95% of GPs have automated offices, and almost 75% use the systems for information sharing of clinical information. In Sweden, 97% of GPs utilize EMRs, and hardly any paper records, prescribing, mostly electronically. It is obvious from the figures that Canada indeed, needs some catching up to do with regard the use by our physicians of healthcare software and ICT in general. The point here is really for all concerned, and in particular, software and healthcare ICT firms to figure out the reasons why there is such disparate in the use of these technologies by family practitioners, who constitute typically, the frontline cadre of professionals in the pathways to health services, between Canada, and countries of comparable economic status. This again highlights the need for these firms to engage in process cycle analysis, as this would help tease out the variety of issues hindering the adoption of these technologies, in the country. That Canadian GPs, and indeed, healthcare professionals in general do not realize the value of these technologies for improving health services delivery is inconceivable[7]. Indeed, it is simply intuitive in many instances and obvious in even more that healthcare information and communication technologies have the potential to improve service deliver, reduce medical error rates, and help in actualizing health education and promotion efforts, including campaigns, and in curtailing health spending. In fact, according to a recent RAND study that Richard Hillestad and his associates conducted, the U.S would save $81 billion annually, including $77 billion from improved efficiency and $4 billion from reduced medical errors, were 90% of healthcare providers to adopt a nationwide electronic health records network[8]. It is also unlikely that Canadian GPs would not support any efforts to assist the country's health system, Medicare, in achieving the dual goals of qualitative healthcare delivery while simultaneously reducing health spending. We need, therefore, to seek the issues involved in improving healthcare software and ICT diffusion, not just among Canadian GPs but also among other healthcare providers, and other healthcare stakeholders, for example, health insurance firms, and the public at large, involved in the different issues and processes that result in the outcome, healthcare delivery.

One major issue in the Canadian health system that healthcare software firms need to pay attention to is that of the public v. private healthcare in the country. This issue has the potential to change not just the dynamics of healthcare drivers in the country, but also their effects on healthcare spending, and by extension, on healthcare software and ICT in general, by all healthcare stakeholders, albeit for different, yet convergent reasons. The burgeoning of niche specialty centers for examples for treating heart diseases, cancer, and orthopedic diseases in the U.S. in recent times exemplifies the stiff competition that would likely follow the entrenchment of private health services in Canada as well, as healthcare providers jostle for competitive advantage developing and marketing profitable specialty-service value propositions to attract clientele. This competition is even going to be keener were software firms, having done their homework, literally, able to offer products and services that could assist healthcare providers in this regard. In other words, we would likely see alliances between healthcare providers and software firms in innovative enterprises for their mutual benefits. Some might argue that while such alliances would move software from the commoditization phase to providing distinct competitive edge, the requirements for the achievement of this goal would itself be an entry barrier, perhaps leaving only the big players in both industries on the turf. However, this is not necessarily a bad thing. Besides the fact that differentiation could occur at different levels in scale and scope terms, that attempts at differentiation could create industry behemoths is just as true as that of its potential for widespread creativity generation, providing opportunities even to the small industry players for market capture. In the context of an industry with literally endless potential for products and services that would help in the prevention and treatment of diseases, and in the promotion of healthy living among others, Canadian software firms, size regardless, have in fact only scratched the market's surface. Canadian software firms, just as their corporate clients in the health industry ought to, should have more than ever, flexible mindsets, and agile business frameworks. They should start to consider how to help their clients achieve the strategic implementation of software technologies into their ongoing operations and processes, both health and non-health related, including with the policy and process reengineering of the organizations operations necessary, in order to gain economic benefits in the short and long terms. Now, this does not apply only to privately funded, healthcare organizations. Medicare, as we noted earlier is reeling under increasing healthcare delivery costs, which is no doubt unsustainable that it needs to embrace the dual healthcare delivery goals of continuing to deliver high quality health services to Canadians while reducing health spending at the same time. Furthermore, many healthcare establishments in the country might need to justify their service provision mix, perhaps even their very existence in the face of "competition" for patients by the private health sector the more established the latter becomes in the healthcare delivery scheme in the country. There is no doubt, that the resulting ethical dilemma would be a main concern government health authorities if it became cheaper in the long term for the health consumer to seek health services in the private health sector, in particular if the latter gained a foothold in providing services Medicare covers. It might well be cheaper to receive those services in the private health sector whose streamlined services and other "private sector" strategic management approaches backed by generous healthcare software deployment, not to mention competition, have resulted in price reduction among others. The healthcare consumer might find it more discerning in terms of costs and convenience for examples, in the long term to use say, the bundled package of products and services mixes that these private healthcare providers might offer. In other words, the coexistence of private and publicly funded health services in Canada might create a scenario where the latter is shedding non-economically viable services, creating the ethical dilemma mentioned earlier as there would no doubt be individuals still unable to afford private healthcare that such moves would adversely affect. One envisages that such service shedding might in fact be necessary for reasons other than competition with a parallel private health system, for example, the emphasis on certain services over others dictated by the exigencies of population changes, or the changing patterns of disease prevalence, among other determinants. Regardless, the need for the public health sector to be goal-focused and to aim for productive transformation to attain those goals is not in doubt. This underlines the need for software firms to offer products and services that would help these organizations add value to their operations via the healthcare software and other ICT that would no doubt increasingly help in enhancing their competitiveness, even among one another, hence averting the ethical conundrum mentioned earlier, among other challenges that contemporary health systems face. It also highlights the need for software firms to embrace the concept of "constitutive" software, rather than merely "enabling" software, which health organizations, including in the public sector would need for such productive transformation. Thus, Canadian software firms would be better poised to exploit the immense opportunities that the healthcare markets have to offer, as noted before, developing innovative products and services based on a thorough process cycle analysis of their markets of interests, analyses that would more likely result in the increasing emergence of such technologies. Since not many small software firms might achieve the initial success and speedy exponential growth in sales, albeit often later slowing down, even while still growing, the firm later becoming a big industry player, nor would want to run into a cash-flow crisis as costs outpace revenues until exhausting working capital, they need to remain in the best survival mode. Indeed, many should consider establishing "niche markets" in the health industry, growing steadily into medium-sized and perhaps forming partnerships and becoming larger firms. They might even prefer ending up acquired by and incorporated into larger firms. The key thing for these smaller software firms, not to forget that they are competing among one another, and sometimes with much larger and better financially endowed firms, hence the need to create distinct value propositions that only a thorough understanding of their markets would guarantee, and again for the process cycle analysis mentioned above. Regardless of what is their "niche", used here in a general sense, which implies essentially a focus on core competencies as organic generics from which other related competencies could emerge, inspired by the strategic intent of assisting their clients' organizations in navigating the transformation process converting capital, material, and human resources inputs for examples into value-added products and services. In other words, that intent alone is sufficient to create the competitive edge the software firms would need to overcome the challenges of the possible competitive benchmarks in the market, regardless of the size of its big players. Thus small-sized Canadian software firms need to ask basic questions such as what services and products to develop, who their clients should be, how they would compete, who or what should be the focus of their strategic intent, and what their measure of success or failure should be among others. In particular, with regard the latter part of the last question, they would probably not want it, but should realize its real possibility and avoid it with calculated vigor, in other words, to know when to change the business model, and move on, before they become moribund. The customary distinction between vertical and horizontal markets being more suited to big and small firms, respectively, is therefore, sometimes blurred, in the health sector, the key point being for the software to be flexible regarding its business model, adapting it to changing market circumstances, ready to capitalize on openings in the market that its comprehensive process cycle analyses reveal. Now, these openings are likely to increase considering the possible implications of the aforementioned dyadic interactions of the public and private health systems in Canada, the latter that already exists, in one form or another, and to a larger or less extent in the country' provinces and territories. Indeed, some argue that the sort of service shedding mentioned earlier is already taking place, with more services not under Medicare coverage any longer in some provinces and territories, and in general less services covered than in even the recent past. The debate on the extent to which government should participate in health services delivery has crucial economic roots besides social equality on the one hand, and adherence to free-market principles on the other. In fact, some neo-liberal economic theorists advocate government involvement on the assumption of the failure of market forces. How is classifying health services and determining resource allocation thereof by economic features such as the nature and extent of information asymmetry, externality, competition, going to affect the nature, pattern, and extent of healthcare software investments in Canada in the years ahead? What would be the opportunities open to Canadian software firms were government to restrict most of its spending to what some in this school of thought refer to as public goods, for example infectious diseases control, immunizations, and other public health-related issues? What if it only focused on regulating health insurance, to ensure equitable access to low-cost private care, colds treatment, say, and in addition to which, financial backing to the poor for high-cost private care, for similar reasons? These approach for example, which Musgrove[9] suggested, while heuristic leaves to conjecture, the nature and manner of the subsidy for the poor for example, which could create the sort of ethical dilemma mentioned earlier. With the need for regulation likely to be less as that for rectifying information asymmetry likely is in an increasingly discerning

Canadian healthcare consumer market, the onus therefore, in preempting the aforementioned ethical dilemma would be on government health authorities to ensure access to health services by the poor via subsidies for the high-costs services. This is in addition to their roles in other health services provision. Canada could relish in its established institutional structures, historical antecedents, and cultural values, factors that in addition to the increasing health spending no doubt would ever more position individual health executive's goals for example in alignment with organizational goals. In other words, the need to ensure access to health services by the poor, and by all other Canadians for that matter, and by extension, that to achieve the dual healthcare objectives would be imperative, necessitating investing in the technologies, for example, that could help in achieving these goals. Part of ensuring that those involved in the delivery of health services adhere strictly to these organizational goals in the health and in fact other sectors would be forging a sense of ownership and involves coupling performance with agreed-upon incentives structures, both of whose underlying issues decomposed, for examples, appropriate buy-in and productivity enhancement, respectively, healthcare software could support. Canadian healthcare software and other ICT firms with change management expertise for example would find ready markets for the former therefore more and more in the near future, as would those that could develop innovative products and services for the latter. Incidentally, these products and services would cover all the issues and processes, health and non-health related, for examples financial, human resources, administrative, clinical, and even technology management, that together constitute the inputs of the transformational processes that result in healthcare delivery. Thus, there would be fewer differences in the approaches to management of the transformational processes by both the public and private health sectors in the near future, and as we have seen, both, albeit for not altogether same reasons, albeit their respective goals converging in the long term, going to need invest more in healthcare software and other healthcare ICT.

Considering the diversity of the healthcare software markets in Canada, the

fast pace of technological progress, changes in disease patterns, and the dynamics between the key drivers of healthcare delivery in the country, among others, what are the likely specific characteristics of and opportunities presented by future health-software markets in Canada? With the increasing applications of software and other healthcare ICT technologies in different domains in the health sector, these opportunities are indeed, immense. There would be an increasing need for example, to rectify the information asymmetry that persists in the health industry on an ongoing basis. The very nature of the healthcare delivery enterprise mandates this. Besides being information intensive, the enterprise is not static, the data, and information it generates, uses, and shares, constantly changing as new medical knowledge emerges from the innumerable scientific researches conducted in hospitals and research centers worldwide. Yet, the trend toward consumer-focused healthcare delivery, and the for those involved in providing this care toward embracing and meeting organizational goals, among others, all predicate on the availability of current, timely, and actionable information. The software and other healthcare ICT that help make this information available would therefore continue to enjoy both niche and mass markets patronage. On the one hand, not even healthcare professionals could hope to keep track unaided by technology, of medical knowledge, considering the magnitude, and speed of developments in their fields let alone in the entire medical domain. They would therefore, also need software that could expedite information retrieval and boost knowledge management, technologies that many institutions now acquire some by subscription, for their staff, and which the professionals acquire individually, too. On the other hand, therefore, the mass markets for such technologies, for example search engines, knowledge discovery and data mining software, and targeted healthcare ICT-enable, and contextualized health information, delivered in a variety of multimedia formats, are immense for the lay public and professionals alike. Canadian software firms need to study the markets and the technologies currently serving them for these tasks, and to decide on the best product/service combo that would capture their markets of interest, be they niche or mass, or even both. To underscore the growing importance of technologies for data and information management in the health sector, Sage Group, an accounting software firm announced on August 09, 2006 that its parent firm is foraying into the health care field. It acquired Emdeon Practice Services (EPS), which develops software for doctor's offices, for $565 million[10], the cash deal billed to close by September, subject to regulatory authorization. Previously known as WebMD, EPS develops and markets practice management and patient data-maintenance software and services mostly to small/medium-sized physicians' offices. With Microsoft's recent acquisition of Azyxxi, database software that collates among others individual patient records, do these acquisitions not give an indication of the interests in these markets and their potential in Canada, also? According to Ron Verni, CEO of Sage Software North America, the company had been interested in acquiring a firm that would enable it offer software products and services to doctors' offices with less than 10 doctors, the size of Sage's core client base. This typifies the points we made earlier about software firms defining their markets, and based on through process analyses, the products and services to offer to these markets, which in Sage's case, was identifying the need of that market of small/medium physician practices for a simple, user-friendly, unified integrated practice management solution for their back-and front-end office processes. Verni also noted that the company has the expertise to develop these products and services, another crucial about coupling the results of process analysis with the software firm's core competencies, or developing/acquiring expertise via partnerships and alliances, and possibly even acquisitions. Most physician practices in Canada are small/medium-sized establishments, and as earlier noted, they are not utilizing healthcare software and other ICT as much as their counterparts in many other developed countries. The markets for innovative products and services for this segment of the healthcare provider market are therefore huge. Targeting such a market underscores our earlier generic usage of the term "niche" market, that is, to encompass both vertical and horizontal dimensions. In other words, Canadian software firms could not only offer specialized products and services for example for GPs' use in accessing and modifying their patients' records on the go, say some sort of remote access software via even their cellular phones, but the software could be adapted for use by the clients themselves to access those records in real time. This would be a variant of the personal health records (PHR), which also contains patients' health history, and to which the client could authorize anyone to view, only this time, the records are the patients' records in the GP's office, to which the owner, the client has real-time access, able to know changes made to entries in the records anytime. Such software would not only serve to reassure clients of the openness of the doctor-patient dyad in the prevailing dispensation, which would encourage them to embrace healthcare software and ICT even more, creating additional business opportunities for software firms, it would empower clients and put them directly in the front seat literally of their health affairs. There is no doubt about the likely interest of the public in such software, nor would there be of the public and healthcare organizations in securing their health data and information, especially in these days of identity theft and more government laws protecting private data. In any case, it is negative publicity that physician practices, and healthcare organizations do not need nor could ill-afford, and as noted earlier the need to build public confidence to promote healthcare ICT diffusion is ongoing. However, the issue of data and information security now transcends securing web servers, or wireless access points, and includes the increasing menace of old computers stacked in warehouses, basements, occupying valuable space in many health institutions, costing storage money, most owners not knowing what to do although in law responsible for the disposal of these computers and storage media. This is a potentially lucrative market, twenty years after the "birth" of the PC by IBM, not least in the health sector. Canadian software firms could no doubt exploit this market offering comprehensive erasure software products and services for processing and destroying data and information irretrievably on hard drives and other storage media. Many healthcare organizations would likely be seeking firms to which to outsource their electronic data and information destruction and recycling tasks, directly or via consultants to recommend waste recycling and reuse vendors of proven integrity, who offer documentation on successful task completion, and whose operations comply with data destruction standards in the country. Indeed, the more the empowerment of healthcare consumers, the greater the choice they have would prove significant in ensuring answerability as organizations become more eager to listen to them and likelier to take the necessary measures to meet their expectations. These measures would no doubt include ensuring the safety and confidentiality of patient data and information, in effect creating immense business opportunities for software firms in all aspects of the security of every aspect of their computer systems, wired and wireless. Canadian software firms interested in the healthcare electronic security markets could expand their value propositions by offering their clients such electronic waste disposal products and services as mentioned above, in addition to those routinely used for computer and network security. No doubt, the security markets will continue to be lucrative particularly in the health sector considering the sensitive nature of the data and information it handles, on the one hand, and the crucial need for data and information communication and sharing in its operations, on the other. Canadian software firms need to be creative in their formulation of ideas, based on the results of their process cycle analyses. They must consider this crucial need by healthcare professionals and patients for access to and safety of information, and exploit the openings in the markets, for example, the need of many users for security software that uses less systems resources, and that cause less system drag. Thus, software firms can simply not overlook the importance of analyzing the markets. In fact, it is not just doctors and their patients that need to keep an eye on health records, other healthcare stakeholders also utilize a variety of information pertaining to their clients' health. It is no surprise therefore that Independence Blue Cross, a major U.S health insurer, is collaborating with 19 other Blue plans across the country to form a huge database of healthcare records that would make it possible for the healthcare consumer, employers, and healthcare professionals to determine what sort of care best suits particular instances[11]. The scheme could also help the participating Blue plans compete more favorably in the market in particular against UnitedHealthcare Group, Aetna Inc. and other major commercial health insurance industry players, who are also offering healthcare consumers more detailed performance data on their healthcare providers including the physicians and the hospitals. Could Canadian healthcare software firms not also explore the private health insurance markets in the country? Would they be able to know the real needs of these insurance firms in the conduct of their business and regarding their relationships with clients, both healthcare consumers and providers, not carrying out thorough process cycle analyses for example? Would the insurance firms, faced with competition, as the above example shows, not be receptive to innovative software solutions that could give an insurance company competitive advantage in the long, even, short-term? As we noted earlier, there would be continuing need to address issues of information asymmetry even in the developed world, as new information emerges routinely and massively in the health sector. The huge databases that the insurance companies are acquiring mentioned above is part of their efforts and indeed, of a countrywide trend in the U.S., to offer health consumers with the information that they need to facilitate their decision making regarding their use of healthcare services. The health insurance consortium for example, could offer useful consumer reports on healthcare and health services simply analyzing real-life data and information on its members, the seventy nine million of them, enabling healthcare consumers to know for example, the primary-care doctors that most often orders which investigations, for example pap smears or which surgeon's postoperative record is best regarding complications. Such information no doubt would help the consumer make up his/her mind about which doctors to patronize. Would Canadian healthcare consumers not also benefit from such information, and could software firms not in fact offer those services developing software that could gather physicians' practice patterns from a variety of sources, including the physicians themselves, and collate such information, including qualifications, malpractice problems, and related issues for offer to the public? There are in fact already physician databases out there, typically compiled by provinces, professional bodies, and licensing authorities, among others, some in fact, available to the public. Could an enterprising Canadian software firm not, perhaps in collaboration with others enrich these databases, and offer them on subscription basis on-line for example, considering that these databases change from time to time? Would such services not outperform the competing databases already on the market, some in CD-ROM and book forms, not readily upgradeable once purchased, the information therein, sometimes lapsing even before reaching the purchaser?

T he Blue Health Intelligence database has all medical procedures and other

care, although has no identifying information on the individual clients. Member plans would access to the databases, which Scott P. Serota, president of the Blue Cross Blue Shield Association in Chicago says, would help change "the present health-care system into a focused, knowledge-based ... system,' in January 2007, provided initially to employers by local insurers, for example, Independence Blue Cross. Doctors and hospitals would also be able to access reports on the quality of care they offer from the insurers, based on strict adherence to widely accepted quality assessments criteria, for example, probing whether the doctor has given heart attack patients beta-blockers, or made certain that patients with diabetes obtained required blood tests and their results promptly. The insurers would release the reports to the consumer following appraisal by health professionals of the quality assurance analysis and techniques, which, according to I. Steven Udvarhelyi, chief medical officer at Independence is "part of our core mission (is) to improve access to high-quality, affordably priced health care…We know that there are quality problems in the health-care system. … We know there is a lot of (practice) variation out there…What we need to understand is what is driving that variation and what can we do to improve quality for our members." Would the insurance companies not need the help of software firms in achieving this goal? Could Canadian software firms not also find out the needs of health insurance firms, or consortia in Canada and develop the products and services to meet these needs? Does this not underscore the need for healthcare software firms to engage in process cycle analyses at various levels to address the many issues in the health and related industries crucial to the achievement of the dual healthcare delivery goals mentioned earlier and by extension to revenue generation by the software firms themselves? Independence hopes for example that its 150-person informatics department that utilizes the firm's own billing data and the all-inclusive consortium database should help it find ways to realize those goals. Could other insurers in both the U.S., and Canada that do not have in-house IT departments not be seeking to outsource these tasks, and would software firms that have the expertise and could in fact offer distinctive value-added services not just fill this gap but outsmart its competition? Further to our suggestion that software firms should conduct process cycle analyses of the issues, the markets, and even the entire industry to determine its products and services, and to be competitive, how would such firms know the various limitations of the database mentioned earlier for example, that its basis is on bills submitted to insurers, not clinical records, otherwise? Could software firms that have conducted process cycle analyses not have discovered this and other issues with this or other databases for example in Canada, for which it could develop solutions to rectify, hence open up a potentially huge and profitable market ? Are there indeed, not markets in the health sector where the need for information and its more valuable utilization is rife in Canada? These examples confirm further the need for a better and fuller appreciation of these markets by software firms in order to discover sometimes cryptic, yet potentially lucrative market opportunities in the health industry, and indeed, in any other. In the U.S., also, Aetna is involved with Care Focused Purchasing, a similar effort that a number of big U.S firms initiated to gather large amounts of health data and information with a view to improving the quality of healthcare delivery. According to Mark V. Pauly, health economist at the Wharton School in the U.S., the Blue Health Intelligence initiative is a rational business strategy considering the current stress on providing healthcare consumers and employers, utilizable information on healthcare delivery quality and the outcome of medical and surgical treatments. This information could even be more valuable, comparing healthcare providers, and health facilities on a variety of treatment, and quality related parameters, perhaps an enhancement software firms could make to the products currently on the market. There is no doubt about the potency of the image issue involved in such data and information, not to mention the prospects of losing clients to better rated providers and health institutions. Would such data and information, therefore not help improve the quality of healthcare delivery in Canada, besides the associated products and services generating income for the software firms involved? Information communication and sharing, as our discussion thus far shows indeed present veritable business opportunities to software firms in Canada, hence worth the necessary exploration to determine the precise products and services that these software firms would prefer to offer the markets. However, these are not the only avenues for revenue generation for Canadian software firms. These firms should also follow developments in the many other domains relevant to the delivery of health services, some health, others, non-health related. In the U.S., for example, such a development was a government auction that started on August 09, 2006, that could trigger the move by many companies, ranging from cable firms to satellite TV providers into the wireless market[12], the quadruple-play service package. Considered the largest spectrum auction by the Federal Communications Commission in ten years, the package that could include wireless voice and data services in an existing bundle of high-speed Internet access, telephony, and television, is sparking intense interest among cable operators and satellite operators alike. FCC is selling 1,122 licenses that the military and law enforcement currently use, the licenses, which cover 90 megahertz of spectrum at 1710-1755 and 2110-2155 MHz, billed to rake in roughly $15 billion. Customary wireless operators, for example, T-Mobile, and nontraditional wireless players, for example cable operators and satellite TV providers, would be hoping to buoy their service packages acquiring these licenses. This would make them better able to compete with major phone firms companies, such as AT&T and Verizon Communications, and to capture significant market share therefore increasing the firms' prospects of increased revenues. Considering the increasingly important role of mobile and wireless technologies in the health sector, this and similar developments should be of interest to software firms, including those interested in the health industry, in Canada. Does the fact for example that satellite providers DirecTV and EchoStar teamed up under the name Wireless DBS to offer U.S $972.5 million bid funds, and cable operators Comcast, Cox Communications and Time Warner collaborated with Sprint Nextel to form SpectrumCo, offered $637.7 million for licenses, not indicative of the massive nature of the markets for these services? In fact, Cingular Wireless and Verizon Wireless, which are essentially awash with spectrum, also made separate deposits to bid on the spectrum, as some experts contend, to raise the entry barrier for the bids, another indicator of the competitiveness of the determination of satellite and cable operators to compete effectively with phone companies. Software firms in Canada ought to be watching these developments with keen interest in particular because of the chances that they would also occur in Canada with the increasing interests by cable and satellite operators in wireless technologies, to boost their bundled service offerings. Thus, they hope that the more services per bundle would increase their chances of competing favorably on pricing, hence rather than reduce prices on individual services, market enhanced packages. Cable operators and satellite firms, which currently lack wireless could therefore, benefit from the additional service offering, participating in what appears to be the emergence of wireless broadband services. It is not difficult to see why the telephone companies are jittery considering that cable operators which seem adept at market capture with their own bundles more than telephone companies are, would now have added services to offer venturing into the wireless domain. In fact, both AT&T and Verizon, which latter incidentally has large stakes in a wireless company of a similar name, conceded that the cable bundle had dented the revenues of their voice enterprises in the second 2006 quarter. Lacking in terrestrial networks it is understandable that satellite firms, many currently in partnerships with phone companies to offer broadband services, although still unable to compete in the latter domain effectively on speed and prices due to the aforementioned lack, need the auctioned spectrum badly. This is more so that the telephone firms could readily jettison them with the ongoing increasing implementation by the phone firms of fiber into their networks as well as improvement in their service offerings, including offering their own TV services. Cable operators also need wireless perhaps less so than satellite operators do though. The former could use it to garner competitive edge as an additional service to what they currently offer, such as customers utilizing a wireless network to program their digital video recorders (DVRs) remotely, or to access their wireless broadband service on the go. There is no doubt that these developments are going to be key drivers of the future of these convergent industries, and with the key roles that software plays in making this convergence work, there is equally none that software firms need already be examining the variety of products and services that they could offer in this regard. Part of the examination involves anticipating how the interplay of the moves by firms in these various domains pans out, the combination of services that they offer and the role that software could play in enhancing them, in a general sense, and in creating new business opportunities for software firms, in the health industry in particular. Perhaps software firms could be looking at assisting those firms that could not obtain additional spectrum in improving their service provision, for example developing software that could manipulate data and voice content hence accelerate transfer speeds, and reduce the strain on computer resources. They might also be interested in developing products that could improve network security including on the increasingly used mobile devices such as cellular phones, and ipods, hence service provision by these other companies.

Some cable operators have collaborated with Sprint Nextel to provide their cable clients a bundled wireless telephone service, hence depend on the latter to access to its network, and the alliance bidding together now on spectrum would increase the authority of the cable companies over their partner's technical infrastructures, and advantage in the partnership, particularly if it crashed. Also of interest, the latest spectrum licenses could enable satellite companies to offer competitive broadband services via such technologies as WiMax, with about 2mbps to 4mbps download capacity, nowhere near that of DSL or cable providers' fixed-line broadband services, but still something. Software companies in Canada should no doubt be aware fully, where all these end up, as many of these firms are also key industry players in Canada. For examples,

Aloha Partners and Qualcomm won most licenses in the first round of auctions for the 700MHz licenses, which wireless broadband operators covet, as it is able to travel longer distances, hence less equipment needed to build networks reducing costs, and to pierce walls. The former firm intends to utilize the spectrum for fixed and mobile broadband Internet services, the latter, its licenses to develop its MediaFLO, the vehicle for offering a wholesale mobile video network to mobile phone firms. Because wireless spectrum is a fixed product, once bought, it is gone, hence the seeming hyper-competitiveness for spectrum auctions, including in Canada. Thus, Canadian software firms should also follow the wireless spectrum scene in Canada, and in particular the backroom moves of its key players nationally, and provincially, such Bell Mobility, incidentally previously only licensed for spectrum in Ontario and Quebec, and Telus, only to British Columbia and Alberta, whose parent firms are the preeminent Telcos in Canada. Others such as Rogers Wireless and Sasktel Mobility are also key industry players, as are some of the multinationals mentioned earlier in the Personal Communications Services (PCS) spectrum licenses that Industry Canada periodically auction. Indeed, Canada also continues to auction spectrum, past auctions for example, facilitating the entry of 3-G compliant wireless devices into the markets with much faster internet connectivity than WAP-enabled phones and personal digital assistants (PDAs,) more spectrum needed as these technologies scale up to 4-G and beyond. With the increasing numbers of mobile devices available on the markets, and of Canadians that own one of more of these devices also, not to mention the likely further increase in their diffusion in the country, the devices, becoming sophisticated increasingly, in functionalities, some cellular phones, now actually doubling as mobile TV the need for additional spectrum could only increase. In the same vein, could only, that for innovative software that are essential elements in the operations of these devices, the prospects of Canadian software firms developing services and products for the health industry channeled through these mobile and wireless technologies truly immense. It is obvious from the above that these auctions are not for the faint-hearted, literally, and that the firm would need to be financially-generously endowed to hope to succeed buying spectrum licenses, which some consider a flaw in such exercises. With respect to the second such auction in Canada, in late 2000, for example, some indeed, contended that an auction in the previous fall in the U.K, which fetched the U.K. government US$56.6 billion, influenced the Canadian auction, from which by some estimated the Canadian government would make perhaps even over $5 billion. This concern regardless, the question remains that Canadian software firms need to know which firms are acquiring which licenses and what they want to do with them and goings-on in general in the industry. For example, they need to be familiar with developments such as the recent announcement by Telus of an exclusive agreement starting in early 2007, to distribute and market mobile gaming, entertainment, information, and messaging services that a California-based firm, Amp'd Mobile Inc, developed. Could software firms not offer health-oriented services and products in association with Telus to the youth market for which these services, accessible only to users of Telus's Wireless High Speed (EVDO) seem tailored? Canadian software firms indeed, should be cognizant of developments in both the private and public sectors in order to appreciate fully the roles that they could play in these industries whose interface with the health industry, and the increasing roles both would play in the future of healthcare delivery in the country, is not in doubt. For example, Industry Canada recently released a gazette seeking comments on 3.6 GHz spectrum licensing by October 27, 2006, regarding its planned policies for licensing spectrum in the 3650-3700 MHz band for wireless broadband applications[13]. It proposed to establish the spectrum policy, technical and licensing provisions to accommodate new Wireless Broadband Services (WBS) in the band. This would be further to the September 2003, *Policy and Licensing Procedures for the Auction of Spectrum Licences in the 2300 MHz and 3500 MHz Bands* subsequent upon which it auctioned 175 MHz in the band

3475-3650 MHz. Then, the Department noted the heightened chances that the U.S. would deploy licence-exempt devices in the band 3650-3700 MHz. It released *Revisions to Spectrum Utilization Policies in the 3-30 GHz Frequency Range and Further Consultation* (DGTP-008-04) in 2004, in which it sought comments on making the band 3650-3700 MHz available for licence-exempt applications, and on the service-types to implement on the band. The comments received supported general synchronization with the U.S. being in Canadians' best interest, but the FCC in 2005 adopted different rules than the planned deployment of licence-exempt devices, to open access to new spectrum for wireless broadband applications in the band 3650-3700 MHz. Hence, the Department seeking the current consultation, the more necessary considering the recent massive auction by the FCC. These comments would likely to influence developments in both the wireless and health industry as the policies would the companies that bid for the spectrum when offered, as would also, what they would be able to do with it, both of which would clearly define to a certain extent the roles that software would play in the services marketed. As we have noted thus far, the need for Canadian software firms to exploit the immense market opportunities in the country is without question, but they need to be cognizant of the variety of issues involved in adopting the right strategic orientation, and in determining the product/service mix that would be profitable in the short, and long terms. As we have also seen, many of these issues on the surface have nothing to do with the health sector, but on closer scrutiny could be even more important in driving the healthcare software market than those directly health-related. Thus, software firms need to conduct the process cycle analysis that we have mentioned numerous times in our discussion, covering both health-and non-health issues. Consider the issue of standards and interoperability for example. These are issues that border on the functioning or otherwise of the software itself, either alone or integrated with legacy and other systems, and are issues that necessitate certain actions by regulatory authorities as the example of the announcement on August 05, 2006, by the U.S. Heath and Human Services (HSS) Secretary Mike Leavitt. The Secretary told the country's governors that the Bush administration would soon oblige all health care providers that receive federal funds to adopt quality-measurement tools and uniform ICT standards[14]. According to Leavitt, President Bush "in a matter of weeks" intends to sign an executive order to create the standards for specific illnesses that would impel the development of uniform approaches to measure and report treatment outcomes, and for four basic healthcare ICT functions. These functions are patient registration, reporting lab results, prescribing, and providing secure communication between patients and doctors and among health care providers, functions very much software related. According to Leavitt, the standards would be a foundation for a health care system that enables patients to make "much more informed decisions", which underscores the point we made earlier regarding the increasing tendency toward patient-driven healthcare delivery in many countries, including Canada. Leavitt also noted that the reformed health system also would result in reduced health care costs and improved patient services, again buttressing our earlier points on the imperative on health services these days, to endeavor to deliver qualitative healthcare while simultaneously reducing health-spending, goals that healthcare software could help to achieve. These issues are also of great import to healthcare delivery in Canada, and require the active involvement of all healthcare stakeholders. It is no wonder then that Leavitt also said that he had consulted with executives from about a quarter of the largest U.S. employers, all of who indicated their intention to sign contracts to implement comparable standards with the hospitals and other providers treating their staff. The Secretary hoped to get more executives on board and urged states to sign such contracts with Medicaid providers, although some of the governors were concerned that doctors might be unwilling to cooperate, a problem that the general disinterest of these professionals in the adoption of healthcare ICT suggests, but which is not necessarily true at least increasingly. In other words, part of the healthcare software and ICT "revolution" involves literally, "winning hearts and minds", which includes determining the reasons for these negative attitudes and doing what is necessary to change them. Thus, as the use by end-users of software is the essential reason for its development in the first place, at least from the viewpoint of the purchaser, the onus is on both the latter and the software developer to ensure that this is the case. The fact is, no one would purchase software eventually if end-user snubbed the products, which could threaten the very survival of the software industry. In short, change management is a major market opening for software firms in particular those with dual business models for example, with consulting services components, in this case, with expertise in change management. Indeed some of the issues that could be hindering the adoption of healthcare software and other ICT by doctors and other healthcare professionals relate to the issues of standards that the imminent laws referred to above are trying to rectify. Without standards, and adherence to them, interoperability would suffer, and without software being able to communicate with one another, they are essentially useless in the health sector and indeed, in general. Canadian healthcare software firms therefore also need to be actively engaged in supporting measures that the relevant authorities in Canada are taking to ensure standards are in place for the seamless integration of disparate healthcare information systems. With regard to doctors in particular, such integration would encourage them to purchase a variety of software for the different tasks, clinical, financial, administrative, that are crucial to the success of their practices, and for collaborating with their colleagues, and indeed, that would link them to the local, regional, and even national health information network, as these evolve. This sort of multi-level integration is the hallmark of a health system that would more than likely be able to meet its dual healthcare delivery objectives. It is also clear, the increased chances of healthcare software firms generating revenues from the incredible market opportunities that would result from such widespread healthcare ICT diffusion. Is it not therefore in their best interests to support such initiatives as those Secretary Leavitt announced, mentioned earlier, and should software firms not adhere to such laws in Canada, too? Canada's health system continues to evolve in many ways. Certainly, we need to deploy healthcare ICT more effectively and ubiquitously. There is little if any doubt that the potential business opportunities for healthcare software firms in the country are substantial and remain largely dormant. We all have a stake in determining what these opportunities are, the benefits that they confer on software firms actually likely to improve the quality of healthcare services that the healthcare consumer receives, and to save the country significant amounts of financial and other resources that it would otherwise expend on an ill populace. In fact, health spending would be even higher under such circumstances as the country's productivity declines and economic growth slows down, which would adversely affect all industries, including the software industry. In the final analysis, therefore, even the healthcare software industry has a stake in recognizing the need to determine the appropriate software products and services that the health industry needs, and to fill the gaps in the market regarding their provision. As we have noted earlier however, these firms would unlikely be able so to do, without the thorough process cycle analysis that would give them the required insight into the real issues in the health industry that need addressing and the technologies, including the software, that could help in doing so.

References

1. Available at: http://www.cbc.ca/story/canada/national/2005/12/07/heatlh-spending-051207.html
Accessed on August 09, 2006

2. Available at:
http://secure.cihi.ca/cihiweb/dispPage.jsp?cw_page=media_10may2006_e
Accessed on August 09, 2006

3. Available at:
http://news.yahoo.com/s/ap/20060810/ap_on_hi_te/ibm_filenet&printer=1;_ylt=Am_jKyCx39.vBjbGTxP2RHtk24cA;_ylu=X3oDMTA3MXN1bHE0BHNIYwN0bWE- Accessed on August 10, 2006

4. Available at:
http://www.medicalpost.com/news/article.jsp?content=20060802_114202_1668
Accessed on August 11, 2006

5. Physician Technology Usage and Attitudes Survey, produced for the Canadian Medical Association and Canada Health Infoway. Available at:
http://www.medicalpost.com/news/article.jsp?content=20060802_114202_1668
Accessed on August 11, 2006

6. Available at:
http://www.medicalpost.com/news/article.jsp?content=20060802_113128_5420
Accessed on August 11, 2006

7. Shekelle PG, Morton SC, Keeler EB. Costs and Benefits of Health Information Technology. Evidence Report/Technology Assessment No. 132, Rockville, MD: Agency for Healthcare Research and Quality, April 2006. Available at: http://www.rand.org/health/feature/2006/060414_shekelle.html Accessed on August 11, 2006

8. Available at: http://www.lasvegassun.com/sunbin/stories/thrive/2005/sep/14/091403227.html Accessed on August 11, 2006

9. Musgrove, Public, and Private Roles in Health: Theories and Financing Patterns. World Bank Discussion Paper No. 339. 1996. World Bank. Washington D.C.

10. Available at: http://news.com.com/Sage+takes+a+565+million+shot+at+medical+software/2100-1012_3-6103845.html Accessed on August 12, 2006

11. Available at: http://www.philly.com/mld/inquirer/15214484.htm Accessed on August 13, 2006

12. Available at: http://news.com.com/Broadband+bundles+to+drive+wireless+spectrum+sale/2100-1039_3-6103519.html Accessed on August 13, 2006

13. Available at: http://strategis.ic.gc.ca/epic/internet/insmt-gst.nsf/en/sf08674e.html Accessed on August 13, 2006

14. Available at:

http://www.medicalnewstoday.com/medicalnews.php?newsid=49049&nfid=al

Accessed on August 13, 2006

Trans-Canada Healthcare Software Business Opportunities

In 2002, the Office of Health and Information Highway (OHIH) initiated a

review of a number of opinion surveys conducted between 1999 and late 2001, aimed at revealing the attitude of health stakeholders for examples, doctors, nurses, pharmacists and health system managers, and of the public, to the use of information and communication technologies (ICTs) in health and health care. This review showed that Canadians although welcomed the role that ICT could play in improving healthcare delivery, had concerns about the ability of these technologies to safeguard their privacy and autonomy, among others, hence advised the need to address these and other legitimate public concerns in order to promote their widespread implementation and use in the health sector[1]. Considering the already high level of ICT penetration in the country, should there be any reason why the applications of these technologies in healthcare delivery should not be equally pervasive, and how much so is it, three years after the surveys, and what could we do to increase their adoption in the health sector? In fact, the survey mentioned above showed that Canadians were keen to embrace healthcare ICT applications aimed at lowering public health risks, tracking medication safety, assessing health trends and improving health information communication and sharing among healthcare providers, with the proviso mentioned earlier regarding privacy and confidentiality of their health data and information. They also would prefer that the use of this information in ways beneficial to health, and with their prior informed consent. Would it therefore not be important for Canadian software companies to pay attention to

119

these concerns, which could be the starting point of strategic product and service development? The surveys showed that health is a priority issue for Canadians, and that many seek health information on the Internet, mostly younger peoples, but also seniors, residents of British Columbia, Alberta and Ontario, most likely, Quebeckers, least likely to do so, and that over 75% of physicians in all age groups use computers, most also Internet users. Should Canadian software firms not tap into this potential market, first fully appreciating to what uses doctors and other healthcare providers put software and other healthcare ICT, the difficulties they encounter in the process, and what improvements they would like to see in these technologies? Would conducting a comprehensive analysis of these and other issues pertaining to their markets of interest not enrich the knowledge of these firms and enhance their decision-making on the most appropriate product/service mix for that market, and their prospects of profitability? Still on the surveys, Canadian doctors most commonly use the computer for research purposes, to surf sites such as Medline, to seek web-based clinical decision-support systems (DSS), and to share information with colleagues over secure e-mail links, including lab and X-ray reports, again, information that is of potential significance for software firms in considering innovative value propositions for this market. Seventy percent of doctors at the time used electronic medical records, and over 50% were involved in professional chat groups, although much fewer, 36% engaged in e-mail communication with their patients. Possible reasons for this latter include lack of coverage of e-mail consultations by provincial fee schedules, and even concerns over information security, issues to which, were some software firms interested in, their exploration could reveal solutions. Specifically, the development of e-mail security software with additional guarantee than current products and services offer, and even proposals to reimbursement authorities, for example, guarantees on checking abuse of e-mail consultations or tracking billing, which might result in policy changes, could be such emergent solutions. The point here is that business opportunities abound in the health sector for Canadian software firms, if only they are willing to apply their resources to the task of ferreting them, as more such opportunities are cryptic than evident. Even those that are obvious would require attention to the issues that surround them as the above examples show, in order to expose the underlying problems and processes that need addressing, hence facilitate the determination of the most appropriate software and other healthcare ICT required to deal with them effectively. Thus, one of the basic measures that Canadian software firms should be prepared to take in order to exploit maximally, the opportunities that contemporary healthcare delivery in the country offer, and all the issues and processes involved in its actualization require is a comprehensive process cycle analysis regarding the issues and markets of interest to the particular firm. Consider the issue of medication costs for example. With health spending in the country soaring, prescription medication costs next in rank only to hospitalizations costs as drivers of these healthcare costs, would finding ways to reduce these costs not be of interest to health authorities in the country considering that spending increasing portions of the country's gross domestic product (GDP) on healthcare provision is unlikely to be sustainable? This, among other reasons is why there is increasing interest of healthcare stakeholders in developments in the pharmaceutical industry, in particular, regarding generic drugs, as an article in the August 15, 2006 edition of the Canadian Medical Association Journal (CMAJ) shows[2]. Specifically, the article mentioned the ruckus following the exposition of enormous rebates to pharmacies, up to 60% of the dollar value of medications sold, from generic drug manufacturers at committee hearings on the Ontario government's Transparent Drug System for Patients Act 2006, the Act itself a subject of controversy. Incidentally, the law itself, passed in late June 2006, underscores the province's quest to curtail the Ontario Drug Benefit (ODB) program's $3.4 billion annual budget, by permitting more usage of generic drugs in place of brand-name drugs. The Act, according to MPP Tim Peterson, expected to make the system "more efficient, more transparent, more accountable, more understandable", in a speech delivered to the provincial lawmakers, has not, however, received unquestioned acceptance by all healthcare stakeholders in the province. Marc Kealey, chief executive officer of the Ontario Pharmacists' Association (OPA), who objected to suggestions that the rebates were not ethical, argued that on the other hand, they are equivalent to volume discounts in a competitive market, where with several generic versions of drugs available, manufacturers compete for pharmacies to stock theirs, based on rebate size. In a sense the more the generics pharmacies stock, the more is available to Canadians, but doctors would still have to prescribe the generics, for one, although pharmacists in Alberta may soon have prescribing powers[3]. Furthermore, would it not even cost ODB much less if it promoted actively, "rational drug prescribing" by doctors since Medicare essentially, health economists would argue, is a prescription for moral hazard. So, besides coaxing doctors to be more "discerning" in their prescribing practice, some of the over-prescribing that likely causes the soaring medication costs in Canada we could do other things about, which is where software firms could not just help the health system save money, but could create immense business opportunities for themselves. Consider that a doctor even needs to prescribe medications, would many over-prescribe if they had an efficient decision support system (DSS) and their practice was evidence-based, the software required readily accessible? In other words, the software firm interested in targeting the market would need to address the slowing of productivity that many doctors that currently use healthcare ICT complain is the reason they shy away from these technologies, as well. What if the software firm was able to develop a DSS that gave the doctor the most current and most appropriate medications for a condition, the doctor keying in the diagnosis and a few other information such as co-morbid medical disorders and allergies, based on the latest research evidence? Some would say that such products already exist, which is true, but do doctors use them, and how frequently, and why not as often as they should? The software firm must have answers to these questions in order to develop a product or service that would outperform current market products, for example, a voice-activated DSS, with the doctor entering fewer data, the required information relayed to the doctor via a wireless earphone virtually invisible to the patient. The above exemplifies the importance for Canadian software firms to conduct process cycle analysis in order to be able to tap maximally, the market potential of the health sector. To highlight the point even further, these firms could also explore the options of developing innovative software to help Canadians prevent illness in the first place, and to promote healthy living, which would be even more effective in reducing medications costs, while opening up a variety of market opportunities for software product and service development. They could also tap into the potentially huge chronic illnesses market, developing products and services for seniors, for example, many with chronic diseases, for the effective treatment and monitoring of these conditions, including on an ambulatory and domiciliary basis, and for the prevention and treatment of their long-term sequelae. Thus, Canadian software firms could conceptualize the issues involved in healthcare delivery from the population health perspective of primary, secondary, and tertiary disease prevention, in making market choices, developing products and services for one or more of these three tiers of this increasingly embraced disease prevention paradigm. By understanding thoroughly the variety of issues involved in actualizing the goals of each tier, it would be much easier for Canadian software firms to determine the required products and services to offer the market and that would be profitable. In other words, in confronting the health sector markets, Canadian software firms need to accept the need for and conduct process cycle analysis, and if unable to do so themselves, outsource it.

The approach to this analysis could vary depending on the strategic objectives

of individual firms, which we must emphasize needs to be modifiable in a market in relatively rapid flux such as the health sector. Nonetheless, and as our example above shows, the software firm might choose to address issues such as medication costs, or others such as hospital wait times and other health services accessibility issues, hospitalizations costs, population aging, geographic spread, or even shortage of healthcare professionals of significance to healthcare delivery in the country. They might also choose to tackle specific diseases, gender, age groups, or medical specialties. They might want to focus on health issues of specific locations, technical issues such as the productivity slowing, and of information confidentiality and security, mentioned earlier, or any of many others for example, systems interoperability. Some of these issues are systems issues, others extraneous to the health system. Some are clinical, others non-clinical, or even health related. The crucial thing is that the software firm needs to tailor its process analysis to its core competencies or to those that could and that it expects to emerge from them in the course of efforts geared toward the achievement of the firm's strategic goals, including from the coalescence of expertise via mergers and acquisitions, for examples. The reason for this is that to compete effectively is to be able to offer products and services that outperform the competition, and how a software firm could do that lacking the required expertise in the first place is difficult to fathom. Thus, the firm would be conducting process cycle analyses on chosen health or non-health issues that on the aggregate result in the outcome, healthcare delivery, the number, nature, and extent of these analyses depending on the individual firm's strategic goals, resources available to conduct the analyses, and a host of other factors. With 40% of the ODB program's share of spending on generic drugs in 2005, $228 million, by OPA estimation, $1.6 billion in all spent on generics in Ontario's public and private markets in the same year, the stakes are no doubt high and the reception by the payers to software that could help reduce these costs unlikely to be hostile. This is more so as the amount of these rebates, incidentally banned in the U.S., some would argue contribute in no small measure to the fact that Canada, according to the Patented Medicines Prices Review Board, has the costliest generic medications among developed countries. Thus, this really would unlikely help, as generic drugs should, in trimming the costs of medications in the province, further highlighting the potential market openings that software firms could exploit in Ontario, and indeed, nationwide, as the issue of increasing medications costs is not peculiar to this province. However, knowing there are opportunities is different from exploiting them, and doing so maximally, which is why the process cycle analysis we mentioned earlier becomes crucial for software firms to perform. Still on the generic medications issue in Ontario, for example, Canadian software firms that intend to offer innovative products and services to the province regarding the generic medications issues ought to appreciate fully the issues concerned. One such issue is Bill 102, which amends the Ontario Drug Benefit Act and the Drug Interchangeability and Dispensing Fee Act. Among its highlights is the appointment of a new executive officer empowered to list new drugs on the formulary, without the need for an Order in Council to approve new listings, as the current protracted and unwieldy procedure requires. Could software firms not help develop software that would facilitate even the operations of the executive officer, who has to act on recommendations from a Committee to Evaluate Drugs, a renamed Drug Quality, and Therapeutics Committee with new consumer/public representation, the software accessible to this committee, pharmacists, and doctors, among other healthcare professionals via a multi-level authentication process? In other words, this software would be "embedded", literally in the processes involved in the use of generics medications, and indeed enhanced to cover all medications, again with differential accessibility policies, for the seamless and efficient operations of the processes involved, rather than "enable" one or the other process. Thus, do software firms interested in addressing this issue not need to understand them fully, and would this not necessitate a process cycle analysis? Would such understanding for example not also perhaps stimulate interest in addressing another feature of Bill 102, the proposed mechanism to replace Section 8, under which Ontario doctors completed 143 370 special application forms in 2004 to obtain prescription drugs not listed in the Ontario formulary, unleashing the creative potential to develop the appropriate software for this mechanism? The Act advocates a new mechanism that allows conditional drugs listings and some exceptional access, the executive officer able to authorize retroactive access and coverage. Could the firm not integrate the software with or actually make it part of a comprehensive, "embedded" system designed to address the various aspects of this issue, including the introduction of a "cognitive service fee" to reimburse pharmacists for professional work, such as patient counseling, another highlight of the bill? The point here is that Canadian software firms would be better able to forge the right strategic direction understudying their markets of interest. Would a firm that does that in Ontario for example not likely understand the health software needs of Ontario, which wants to save money by putting pressure on the price of generics, the government intent on negotiating agreements to pay generics 50% of the price of the off-patent brand-name product? Does this not indicate that the province is keen addressing the generics issue, and could other provinces and territories not also be interested to do so, and should a healthcare software firm that wants to exploit fully the enormous potential of the country's health sector markets not want to know? Would what such a firm discovers unlikely to coincide with the aspirations of the province or territory, hence the likely future spending oh healthcare software and other ICT? Could such analyses not in fact reveal opportunities in both vertical and horizontal markets? Still on the generic medications issue in Ontario, as noted earlier, the province also plans to ban "rebates" but allow pharmacies to receive, from generic manufacturers, 20% of the listed drug cost as a "professional allowance", a code of conduct developed, with OPA input, on spending the 20%. However, this prohibition would not apply to drugs bought under employer-sponsored health plans or by persons paying out-of-pocket for their medications, and as for corporate plans, the prices listed in the formulary, used as the benchmark price. Would the province not need a system to monitor, and enforce this prohibition, and could a software firm not develop the software for such a system? Could this software also not be an integral part of the overall "embedded" solution for the generics, and perhaps even prescription medications management issues? Would the software firm that understands these issues best and that knows the specific goals that the province wants to achieve not develop the most appropriate software solutions, hence be far ahead of its competitors in the market? Could experience and market advantage gained in Ontario not stand this company in good stead in seeking similar projects in other provinces and territories? Do these perquisites not underscore the need for Canadian software firms to engage in process cycle analyses for their markets of interest? Even those that welcomed many of the changes proposed regarding the generics issues in Ontario agree that many issues remain unsettled, and would perhaps remain so until the publication of the rules in October 2006. Does this not suggest that interested software firms would need to keep abreast of developments on this issue? Indeed, it also underlines an important point that the health sector is in a state of perpetual flux, as indeed, other industries are. The significance of this point regarding the software industry is that healthcare delivery could never be perfect, due in the main to this flux, the possibility of changes within and without the health sector mandating perhaps even paradigm shifts in healthcare delivery. Thus, we would need to continue to seek new solutions in light of these changes, and of our ongoing quality assurance exercises, breaking down specific issues in order to expose their underlying issues and processes, in an endless decomposition/exposition process, taking the appropriate action, barring any psychological fallacy, to modify the processes as required. Accordingly, it is important for software firms to appreciate the fact that process cycle analysis necessarily would be a continuous process, to move the health system closer to perfection. In the case of Bill 102, it is in the interest of all stakeholders for its propositions to succeed, and as noted Jim Keon, President of the Canadian Generic Pharmaceutical Association, "We're quite concerned...We won't give our support until we see and understand how the regulations will work, a stand that the brand-name industry is also taking, as its Rx&D spokesperson, Jacques Lefebvre, also noted. These comments also should suggest to Canadian software firms that the market for software that could make the laws work is there, waiting.

A s we mentioned earlier, the choice of issues, province, territory, or any component of any other taxonomic criteria a software firm used to approach its strategic initiatives in any market would depend on each firm's goals embodied in its vision and mission. Thus, a firm might be interested in Ontario and in some particular health issue in the province, or none at all, but seeking to know on which it should. In other words, the process cycle analysis of the former firm would be specific, and that of the latter more broad-based. Nonetheless, it would be ideal for both to have a general idea of the healthcare software markets in the province, and in relation to those of other healthcare ICT. Ontario for example is keen expressly to improve its ability to collect more accurate, current health information, which it expects to facilitate the management of data, and information management generated by health care providers, for examples hospitals and Community Care Access Centers, hence that of tracking and monitoring the healthcare system's performance, and accountability. Clearly, software firms could explore these goals and the issues surrounding their actualization, hence able to develop innovative products and services to help in doing so. In other words, software firms could work with the province in realizing its strategic focus to tackle the system-wide need for more effective information management, namely, "producing better data, supporting accountability, and quality improvement through performance measurement, and supporting evidence-based decision-making[4]". The province also intends, in attaining these goals, to establish improved standards for data quality, and the seamless integration of data from disparate sources, into a consolidated knowledge base, accurate, real-time information made available to healthcare providers to enhance service delivery at the point of care (POC.) As broad-based as these goals sound, they contain the essential elements of what the province wants to achieve, hence on what health software and other healthcare ICT it would likely be interested to acquire and implement, hence crucial for software firms to decipher the details of these goals, which they could by engaging in process cycle analysis. Thus, there is no doubt about the need for software that would facilitate information sharing among healthcare professionals, such as EMRs in physicians' offices integrated in a province-wide electronic health records (EHR) systems, the software firm under this circumstance actually able to choose between exploring either the horizontal or vertical dimension of this particular issue, or in fact both. In other words, software firms could develop products and services, or improve upon those currently on the markets for either of the individual doctor's office or for the provincial health system or both. Clearly, considering the costs of these systems, which could be quite high for all-inclusive packages for the former, and for the latter, too, software firms could consider developing components of say EMRs, for those practitioners financially challenged, hence only capable of incremental implementation of the system. This might be what some health authorities or bodies within the province might also be able to do for similar or other reasons. Standards and quality appraisal also seem to be paramount goals of the province hence would likely be keen on software that would facilitate its being able to measure accurately and track the performance of the health system, and that would enable its residents to assess the system's quality and progress. This means the government is likely keen for its residents being able to access certain important quality dimensions such as adverse events reports, accreditation reports and status, performance statistics of both healthcare professionals and hospital facilities, and audit reports, among other valuable information. These are no doubt important openings for software firms to develop appropriate products and services, here again, for either or both vertical and horizontal markets. To underscore Ontario's attention to health information management, it appointed as Lead for Information Management for the government's Health Results Team in September 2004, to spearhead its efforts, Adalsteinn (Steini) Brown, an Assistant Professor in the Department of Health Policy Management and Evaluation at the University of Toronto and the principal investigator for the Hospital Report Research Collaborative. The province has also established, among others, the Health System Intelligence Project (HSIP), a team of health system experts that the Ministry of Health and Long-Term Care's (MOHLTC) Health Results Team for Information Management (HRT-IM) retains as part of the government's overall Information Management Strategy to complement and augment its current analytical capacity. The team provides the Local Health Integration Networks (LHINs) with refined data analysis and interpretation and with staff training in these processes using novel techniques and technologies, again openings for product/service development that software firms might want to explore. Furthermore, as the team collaborates with MOHLTC analysts to secure crucial analytical support for the local health system planning initiatives of LHINs, including the acquisition and implementation of healthcare software and other healthcare ICT that they need to improve health services delivery, it is important for software firms know of goings-on among these different bodies. In its "Scio-Economic Indicators Atlas" for Erie St. Clair LHIN published in spring 2006, for example[5], HSIP noted the substantial variation between and even within its 25 Census subdivisions (CSDs), an area that is a municipality or deemed to be equivalent to a municipality for statistical reporting purposes, the variations not just in size, especially in the LHIN's urban centers. According to 2001 estimates, the area of the Erie St. Clair Local Health Integration Network (LHIN) had 609,700 people, or 5.3% of Ontario's population1, the CSD population ranging from 300 (less than 1% of the Erie St. Clair population) to 208,400 (34.2%)[5]. There are also notable differences in age structure, economic situations, and social features, all not just with implications health status and for health services planning, but also for the nature and extent of the healthcare software market. Versus the entire province of Ontario, for example, a higher percentage of the Erie St. Clair LHIN population are 65 years of age and older, have not completed a high school education, and the percentages for recent immigrants, visible minorities, and of economic families living below the low income cut-off are lower, according to the report. Such information in combination with others such as the prevalence and types of chronic diseases, the number and types of community living services, and the nature and extent of ambulatory and domiciliary care in the area, could indicate possible software products and services to develop for horizontal markets in the area. As we noted earlier, it is important for software firms to choose and explore issues and markets of interests in the health sector. One such issue is that socio-economic status (SES), which no doubt is an important determinant of health and there is equally no doubt about the connection between health status, health services use, and SES[6, 7]. Socio-economic drawback has strong links with inequalities in health, life expectancy, and quality in general directly proportional to income, the unemployed, and their families more prone to premature death, and low education levels linked with riskier health behaviors[8]. The population health perspective mentioned earlier acknowledges the significance of these connections, hence the need for such factors as social, economic, and physical milieus, personal health practices, individual capacity, coping skills and health services[9, 10]. Software firms need to appreciate the interplay of these variables in their markets of interest, the relative socio-economic handicap of these markets versus others at least in the province. They need to know, for examples, the potential effects of variables such as income and education levels, housing, immigration, employment/unemployment, family characteristics, aboriginal status, and language, among others on disease patterns and prevalence and on health risks in general. Such information would be helpful in characterizing the market from a health perspective, and for determining the appropriate product/service mix for any of say the issues pertaining to the population health primary, secondary, or tertiary multi-level, disease prevention paradigm in the chosen markets. The more the elderly that live in an area for example, the higher the likelihood of chronic health conditions, the higher the utilization of health services, and just to mention one or two examples, regarding healthcare software, the likelier would the need for software for ambulatory and domiciliary care, including assistive healthcare technologies. Family composition is also important, single parenthood for example having potential health implications. For example, single-mother family status is a major predictor of cumulative mental health problems, income, gender, family size, education, and personal psychosocial features of the parent, controlled for[11]. Aboriginal Canadians are higher risks for Diabetes Mellitus for example[12], and immigrants and visible minorities, lower income status, higher unemployment rates, and hence higher risks of ill health in general[13]. This again, is information that could result in further decomposition and exposition in order to understand the underlying issues and processes better, which could make it easier to determine what healthcare software to offer the respective market.

A software firm interested in vertical markets should want to know for example, what information holding its province or territory currently has, what they do with the database, who is able to access it, how integrated it is with other holdings, and government's plan for additional holdings. Provinces, territories in Canada, the federal government, and its various health agencies already have extensive databases, organized in a number of different categories, for examples, clinical, demographics, financial, human resources, reference, surveys, and so on. Other classifications are along health and non-health subjects, for examples regarding the former, services such as acute care, emergency care, palliative, care, community care, long-term care, mental health/addictions, complex continuing care, primary care, and rehabilitative care. Other health subjects include wait times related information holding such as cancer services, knee/hip replacement, cardiac services, MRI/CT scan, and cataract services. Yet others are demography-based such as according to age groups, with separate databases on children, youths, adults, and seniors. Other databases focus on a variety of issues such as diabetes, women's issues, pediatrics, osteoporosis, trauma/injuries, patient safety, prescription drugs, morbidity, and mortality. Thus, the software firm has a wide range of subjects from which to choose that is keen on vertical markets. An analysis of the chosen subject would reveal no doubt the issues involved that need addressing, the status of competition in the market, and the prospects for the software firm of competitive advantage developing which product/service mix. The issues might in fact cut across different information holdings or subjects, for example, that of standards and interoperability, information safety and security, and authentication issues, all areas, among others of immense potential market opportunities in virtually all provinces and territories in the country as well at the national level. Such analyses would also reveal to the software firm, the areas that a province or territory would likely be investing healthcare software funds on and their healthcare ICT priorities in general, at least in the short, and indeed, in the long terms. In Ontario for example, the province has immense technological capabilities in data and information gathering and collation, and large volumes of health-related data and knowledge base, and is gathering even more via key government initiatives for example, the Wait Times Strategy and the E-Health Strategy. Thus, the province is collecting new patient data to track wait times and to enable the creation of electronic health records (EHR), data that will ultimately require consolidation, hence clearly a potential area of healthcare software need. Furthermore, new institutions such as the Local Health Integration Networks (LHINs) will in the near future need to access these massive data and information repositories. The core of the province's Information Management Strategy is meeting the increasing needs fro access to these databases, integrated and all-inclusive. Indeed, as part of its efforts to meet these needs, the province has mapped out the value chain of health information as at September 2004 as Figure 1 shows.

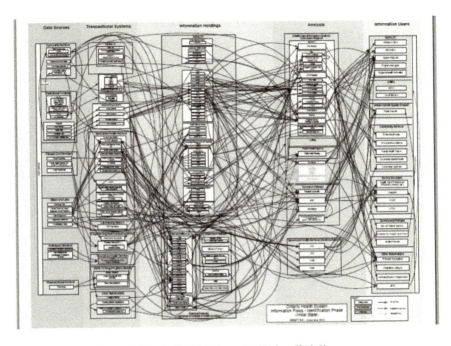

Figure 1: Ontario Health Information Value Chain[14]

The map shows how information travels across the province's health system from its origin, when first collected, to its eventual destinations including the variety of end users who use it, for clinical or non-clinical purposes foe examples, decision-making, research, health planning, or policymaking. The province's comprehensive analysis yielded valuable results, and in fact, it developed a blueprint for the future state of information management in the province as shown in Figure 2, a more organized, efficient, effective, and eventually more longer lasting and cost-effective, health information management. Indeed, the province envisages this improved management throughout the information's entire life cycle as it aims to fulfill the information needs of healthcare professionals, system analysts and planners, and of hospital managers, executive, and decision makers, and indeed, of all healthcare stakeholders in the province.

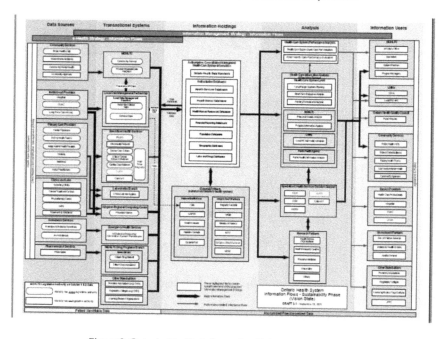

Figure 2: Ontario Health Information Value Chain[15]

There is no doubt about the value of software firms to understand fully, the various elements of the province's information management strategy if they wanted to succeed in doing business in its healthcare software business sector. Thus, and as figure 2 shows, they need to know the potential business

136

opportunities derivable from the actualization of major elements of the strategy such as at the healthcare provider level, reducing the burden of data collection and reporting via data rationalizations, which entails cutting out unnecessary, low quality or value data and information, and filling information fissures. Software firms should, based on this goal, be considering developing the appropriate products and services to help with achieving them cost-effectively, of course after a thorough process cycle analysis to understand further the underlying issues and processes as previously described. The province wants to create alliances, at a local level, among healthcare providers with the goal of improving data quality and the currency and promptness of reporting via best practices, standards, and tools, for examples, again, clear indications of the sorts of software and indeed, healthcare ICT in which the province would likely be investing in the near future. Further, at the system level, the province is keen on data integration essentially first in recognizing authoritative information holdings, then in their virtual and/or actual integration, and the purging of duplicate and minimal-value data and information, which promises probably extensive business opportunities for system integrators, interoperability software and other technologies, and database management firms, among others. The province also wants to develop more analytical capacity to support planning and decision-making at all levels, local, intermediate, and system-wide, and to integrate and align the province's health system around major health strategies and performance measures to encourage and ensure the sort of perpetual performance and improvement we mentioned earlier. It is obvious how much software firms could achieve in terms of business opportunities in Ontario conducting process cycle analyses on these various health-information management goals of the province, the same principles, and likely outcome applicable to other Canadian provinces and territories, and at the federal level. With data on the utilization and efficiency of hospital care in Ontario, for example, taking over eight months to process, as it took forty years ago, the province having over a hundred individual health information databases, many containing identical data and unable to communicate with one another, it is not difficult to understand the province's health information management goals. Furthermore, with almost 2,000 individual performance indicators, an indicator evaluating the performance of some aspect of the health system, for example, surgical wait times, many such indicators of limited use either hard to administer or interpret, hence offering equally limited information, or that with no clear benefits or relevance to the government's major health concern, the goals are sound. Software firms could no doubt apply their resources in an exercise, the process cycle analysis we have highlighted so far, to figure out the appropriate products and services for these gaping markets, for example, to help streamline data reports, some 200 separate ones that the typical hospital in the province submits, some daily, making the process more efficient and cost-effective. We have used Ontario to illustrate some of the principles key to success in the contemporary healthcare software markets in Canada, although we need to emphasize that they also apply to the other provinces and territories. In other words, software firms need to appreciate the issues that surround healthcare delivery in whichever provinces or part of which province or territory it is interested to explore. There are of course likely to be differences between these provinces and territories in many respects, but these differences are unlikely to obscure the commonalities in their overall healthcare goals, in keeping with the ideals of the Canada Health Act, its five principles namely, public administration, comprehensiveness, universality, portability, and accessibility, on the one hand. On the other, is the obligation of the provinces and territories, legal this time, as the Act lays down the criteria and conditions essentially, the national standards for insured health care services, which they must meet to receive the full federal cash transfer payment under the Canada Health and Social Transfer (CHST).

Governments all around the country are investing in healthcare software and

a variety of healthcare ICT to achieve their healthcare delivery goals, and with the increasing need for these governments to meet the dual healthcare delivery objectives of providing qualitative health services to their residents at the same curtailing soaring health spending, these investments could only increase over time. As we have noted, they approach these investments based on their immediate, short-and long-term health services priorities, which could be system issues, clinical issues, or even exigencies issues that address certain crises. On July 12, 2006 for example, Residents of Strathroy and nearby communities, received approval for a new CT scanner for Strathroy Middlesex General Hospital, according to an announcement by Ontario's Health and Long-Term Care Minister George Smitherman, facilitating access to diagnostic services[16]. Noted the Minister, "People suffering from significant health problems should not have to wait long periods of time to be diagnosed...This new machine will mean that more people in this area will receive the diagnostic procedures they need closer to home". In this instance, the technology would be solving service accessibility issues, and would likely be creating opportunities for software firms to offer a variety of products to enhance its functionalities for example, picture archiving and communications systems software, and other image and practice management software. With the new CT scanner at Strathroy Middlesex General Hospital expected to deliver 4,300 additional scans per year for the residents of Middlesex whose population grew by almost 10% between 1996 and 2001, these opportunities are quite substantial, and with the scanner billed to be operational in the spring of 2007, software firms could certainly still exploit these opportunities. Incidentally, opportunities for offering image and practice management software are not limited to new CT scanners or similar imaging technologies only when new, as there are prospects to offer sophisticated products and services with enhanced features that make them more efficient and cost-effective than the software the thousands of CT scanners all over the country currently use. This again, underscores the need for software firms to do some research and analysis, which if they could not themselves do, should outsource, the market opportunities that might open up thereafter likely to outweigh the costs they incur conducting these analyses. In Southwestern Ontario alone, the McGuinty government has several initiatives that would need healthcare software input in many ways, for example, increasing access to doctors and nurses via 150 new Family Health Teams province-wide, including 15 in the South West Local Health Integration Network (LHIN), access that software to improve information communication and sharing would no doubt facilitate. It also invested about $9 million in new funding for improved home care via community care access-centers including $958,200 for community support services in the South West LHIN, again, an initiative that would require heavy healthcare software and ICT involvement to facilitate. The government is also investing more than over $40 million on increasing services and lowering wait times in five major areas namely, hip and knee joint replacement, cataract surgeries, MRI/CT exams, cancer surgeries and cardiac procedures. This investment includes more than $12 million for an additional 28,392 MRI and CT scans in the South West LHIN alone, which underlines the point we made earlier about the significant investments ongoing, in many provinces in Canada, on healthcare ICT including healthcare software. According to the Health Minister, "Patients expect and deserve the best possible health care…We are providing Ontarians with faster access to better health services, to reduce their pain and suffering and keep them healthier, longer." With such stated commitment to health service provision, and plan for innovation in public health care to build a system that delivers on three priorities, namely keeping Ontarians healthy, reducing wait times, and offering improved access to healthcare professionals, should software firms not be seeking to understand the province's health system better? Should they not be conducting process cycle analyses to achieve this understanding, which would enable them to determine the software to offer the immense market opportunities in the province's vertical health sector markets? To highlight further the commitment of the province to reducing hospital wait times and improving accessibility to health services, the Ontario Ministry of Health and Long-Term Care will be implementing a surgical performance feedback service, McKesson's OR Benchmarks Collaborative, in Ontario hospitals[17]. This initiative is a component of its Surgical Targets Program to reduce wait times for cancer, cardiac, cataract, hip, and knee surgeries on the one hand and to rationalize resource utilization, in effect, to achieve the dual healthcare delivery goals of improving services and reducing costs simultaneously. Over the next few months, 80 hospitals and 14 integrated delivery networks in the province will have access to the service, which also underscores the potential markets for not just software products but also required services in the health sector. In this instance, benchmarking services, as Lorraine Osbourne, a sub-contractor with the Ontario Ministry of Health leading seminars for the selected hospitals' staff members, noted, "(the service) brings concrete data, alleviating the question about where the time issues are…The whole province is looking at wait time problems. Hospitals are canceling patients' everyday due to inefficiencies in the operating room", are of increasing interest among healthcare providers. This particular initiative requires hospitals first submitting to a McKesson-customized website, the information for up to 21 categories that include post-operation login, commencement time accuracy, and procedure codes, then they could track their performance over time including relative to that of other hospitals, and could drill down to discover any issues pertaining to their operations. They could therefore, readily identify issues that need addressing, which would no doubt in many cases require the use of cutting-edge software to facilitate operations, again, the potential market openings for software firms, likely huge. OR Manager, the New Mexico-based benchmarking services provider launched, in association with McKesson, these services in January 2006, with already over a hundred subscribers in both Canada and the U.S., which attests to the variety of unmet service needs in the health sector that software firms could discover conducting thorough process cycle analyses. As with hospitals in Canada, U.S hospitals are also keen to improve surgical efficiency, Cedars-Sinai Hospital in Los Angeles, one of the many that utilize an OR data management system that facilitates the tracking of hospital efficiency. This is going to be an increasingly important aspect of healthcare delivery, and as M. Michael Shabot, MD, medical director of enterprise information services and surgical intensive care at Cedars-Sinai noted, "If you can't measure it, you can't improve it…It is important for hospitals to use optimally very expensive resources such as this [OR data management] technology." Indeed, the American College of Surgeons has offered, to its members since October 2005, a case log system for its members to key in surgical data into their PDAs or on the Internet. The data and information submitted including the procedure, diagnosis, and conditions of the surgical procedure, allowing, as Shabot put it, "the surgeon to compare his or her own cases with peers completely anonymously", 25,000 cases logged since the inception of the system, which Shabot envisages would provide specialty-specific data for its members in the future. Here again, is an example of the many issues relating to health care delivery that software firms would not know about, let alone realize that they offer potential market opportunities if they did not seek them out, via conducting the comprehensive process cycle analyses that we have so much talked about in our discussion. These analyses themselves must predicate on information about the status of health services in the province or areas of interest. In other words, software firms need to have a general knowledge of healthcare services in the province or territory of interest to know the issues germane to healthcare delivery there. To use the example of Ontario again, the province designates some communities as under-serviced in an ongoing self-evaluation process subsequent for example, upon communities identifying themselves to the MOHLTC as in need of assistance for the recruitment and retention of healthcare providers, and upon meeting certain criteria. The Ministry may designate communities in the province for General/Family Practitioners (GP/FPs) if experiencing a major doctors' shortage, although only northern communities qualify as underserviced for specialists. For a community designated as underserviced, practice opportunities appear on a List of Areas Designated as Underserviced (LADAU), distributed to health professionals keen on working there. Knowledge of these areas would be useful for example, to software firms that could offer inventive products and services that could facilitate health service provision in such areas such as tele-health and other remote practice technologies for consultation, diagnosis, and even treatment both acute and long-term, of a variety of health problems. Canada has many such remote and difficult-to-reach areas in virtually every province and territory, more so in the territories, where such products and services have even more extensive markets. Saskatchewan, for example, has a Northern Telehealth Network, a consortium of Saskatchewan Health, SaskTel, and six Saskatchewan health districts, which represents those districts serving remote and rural communities with First Nations populations. The consortium also represents regional health centers that act as referral and secondary treatment sites, and an urban tertiary referral and specialist centers. Recently it received $489,700.00 from Health Infostructure Support Program (HISP) to fund a project: Tele-Health Infrastructure Enhancements - Northern Tele-Health Network, whose objectives are to improve access to health services from remote areas as well as to health related education and information for both health providers and consumers[18], enhancing the pilot Northern TeleHealth Network activities. Telehealth utilizes cutting-edge communication and multimedia technologies to offer a wide range of services to patients in a number of medical fields including dermatology, orthopedics, child psychiatry, radiology, obstetrics, pediatric surgery, plastic surgery, psychology, counseling, diabetes management, and Acquired Brain Injury consultation, among others. Software firms with interest in these technologies and upon a detailed exploration of the needs of each area of medicine would emerge equipped with the information to determine and develop products and services for these still-burgeoning markets, which as we noted earlier are countrywide. Besides tele-health, on which the province continues to invest substantially, it is also investing a number of different healthcare ICT programs. In its 2004/2005, annual report, the Saskatchewan Health Information Network (SHIN) since the same period, an agency of the new Health Information Solutions Centre (HISC) at Saskatchewan Health, noted that it established the Saskatchewan Surgical Patient Registry, the first such system in the country, HISC developing the IT[19]. This is part of the province's efforts to manage wait lists better and improve access to health services, the registry, in which other provinces and territories have shown keen interest, which utilizes a groundbreaking information capture technique, on patients awaiting services province wide, facilitate the effective management of surgical wait times and of resource allocation and utilization. In the period under consideration, the use of SHIN's provincial network increased by 20%, even higher regarding the number of service points that technologies for telehealth and renal dialysis enabled, services that improve the access to care in remote parts of the province and which create immense business opportunities for healthcare software firms. SHIN extended the reach of its home care system to another three health regions (Keewatin Yatthé, Kelsey Trail, and Mamawetan-Churchill River) in 2004/05, ten regions now utilizing this new system and it implemented, a central patient index system in the Prairie North Health Region (North Battleford), and the first transcription system in the Sunrise Health Region. This same period witnessed further work on setting up the basis for the electronic health records (EHR) program in the province, which even now is a veritable source of market opportunities for software firms interested in the horizontal healthcare software markets. The province continues to invest, through SHIN, in the technologies crucial to building on work done so far on the network, including a care provider information systems core, the foundation for the development of EHR solutions province-wide, essentially opening up a huge EMR-technologies market in the province. Indeed, SISC via SHIN is collaborating with Canada Health Infoway (Infoway), on a variety of projects to accelerate the development of EHR systems in the province, the partnership yielding $4.5 million to advance the implementation of province-wide EHR solutions in the year in question, for Client and Provider Registry, Pharmaceutical and Diagnostic Imaging Information system projects. The province received another $15.5 million in late 2005 for its EHR program, to start a number of new projects and to quicken existing ones, the first phase of projects in the EHR program, for example, the Pharmaceutical Information Program, billed for implementation in 2006. Planning for other projects, for example, Diagnostic Imaging and Laboratory will also accelerate in 2006, again with positive implications for business opportunities for software firms.

O ther provinces and territories are also investing substantially on healthcare

information and communication technologies. In Quebec, for example, reducing wait times and improving accessibility to health services are major issues of concern, particularly in the context of the ruling by the Supreme Court of Canada on June 09, 2005 in the *Zeliotis/Chaoulli v. Quebec* case that the Quebec government cannot stop people from paying for private insurance for health-care procedures that Medicare covers. In other words, Québécois could now access health services in the public and private sectors[20], which inherently creates additional market openings for healthcare software firms, as the option of private-sector health services access would trigger competition among providers in that sector as they jostle for patronage. This competition is likely to lead to the quest for differentiation to gain competitive edge, which again, intrinsically creates room for software firms to offer valuable products and services to help healthcare providers achieve their goals. In fact, this competition is unlikely to be just between private healthcare providers, but would also be between them and the public health sector, which latter might need to justify the economic viability of some of its services and facilities under such circumstances. Hence it would need to make some structural adjustments, including shutting some facilities down, merging others, the province's controversial complementarity principle perhaps indicative these are already happening, and strengthening yet others, where software and other healthcare ICT would no doubt play distinctive roles. Quebec, as other provincial and territorial governments, sticks to the general principles for reducing wait times and improving the access time to quality health care and services, as the Prime Minister and provincial and territorial premiers stated at the Conference on Health Care in September 2004. Quebec's priorities also include providing specialized treatments and services in cancer, heart, medical imaging, joint replacement, and sight restoration. The province's commitment to improve access to services, for which it confronted how to manage wait times, that is to develop and implement the tools and mechanisms for improved service access management to ensure patients receive the services they need. It also faced the issue of cutting down wait times, when objectionable, which involves first setting wait-times limits based on clinical evidence and priorities, and has been investing significantly in healthcare ICT in a determined effort to solve both problems and would likely continue to do so. In January 2004, for example, regarding access to services in the tertiary cardiac and radio-oncology sectors, the Ministère de la Santé et des Services Sociaux implemented, in every health institution in Quebec offering tertiary cardiac services, the standardized service access management system (SGAS, système de gestion de l'accès aux services). It implemented a similar system in September 2004, expressly for radio-oncology in institutions providing radio-oncology services[21]. The province intends to continue to optimize the use of expensive technologies while assuring ready access to the services they offer, a key objective that healthcare software needs to explore further to be able to develop and offer appropriate healthcare software that would assist in its achievement. For example, the province would certainly want to improve on its successes in this regard achieved by every healthcare institution adopting a uniform list of priorities for service requests based on a morbidity and mortality risk scale that experts in each specialty defined by consensus, which, further to noticeably improving wait time management, helped produce quality standardized information management. It would in fact also want to replicate these successes in other priority areas for examples, medical imaging, sight restoration and joint replacement, for which it is yet to implement an SGAS type standardized service-access management system to enable full patient follow-up while awaiting services based on their needs. There is no doubt that work is ongoing on implementing more cutting edge information technologies to improve wait times and that the province would embrace software and other healthcare ICT that would enhance even those already implemented. The onus is on software firms to offer such products and services, for examples that would improve services organization and standardization, analyze and interpret wait times on a regular basis, improve the mechanisms for patient preparation and checkout, and address other important issues and processes concerning wait times. Thus, and as we noted earlier, software firms need to engage in process cycle analysis, for them to appreciate fully, these issues and their underlying processes, hence be able to develop the required software to address them successfully. Quebec continues to invest in a variety of high technology equipments for which the need for software is not in doubt. For examples, in 2005-06, in addition to the 13 MRIs it has currently, the province plans to acquire 37 more, and in addition to the three CT scanners being set up, it plans to acquire 98, more, and four more

PET, including the one it has now. The Ministère recognizes that for its various initiatives to reduce wait times to succeed requires the involvement and commitment of all network parties, the specialists concerned, included, and of course the GPs and other referral sources, among others, which clearly suggests the need for information communication and sharing and for data integration among these parties. This also points to the likely increasing need for the appropriate software and other healthcare ICT to enable and facilitate these links, market opportunities that enterprising software could exploit maximally understanding fully, the interplay of the many issues and processes involved in achieving these information and data integration goals. Because of the increase in the aging population in Quebec, which incidentally is greater than in any other province or territory in the country, the province would continue to experience an increased demand for health and social services. Hence, the likelihood of the health authorities embracing more and more, the healthcare software and other ICT that could assist in delivering health services to its seniors is undeniably high. This is more so that there is a decrease in the number of young persons keen in the health and social services network, thereby replacing the seniors that are retiring, including healthcare professionals. The demand in both the horizontal and vertical markets for software that would enable ambulatory and domiciliary treatment of seniors' health issues would likely increase significantly in the province. This is evident in its adoption of the *Home Support Policy "Home is the Option of Choice"*, made public on February 21, 2003, and in its allocation in the 2004-2005 budget, $61 million extra for home support, or 30% of the $200 million allotted for new public services, the bulk, $50 million, allotted to senior citizens who have lost autonomy. Thus, the demand for these technologies would perhaps increase even more than it would in the other provinces and territories. However, the technologies would be in high demand in general for the management of chronic health problems even among younger individuals. Software firms interested in tapping these markets would need to study the market of interest in the location of interest as we have advocated thus far. This would reveal the nature and extent of the health problems, the availability or otherwise of providers, and the accessibility, in general of residents to health services, among other factors that would help the firms in determining which products and services to offer the chosen markets. Coupled with its relentless recruitment and retention initiatives, and its adoption on December 18, 2003, Bill 30, which facilitates human resources management, including resource allocation and utilization, the right technologies could indeed, alleviate the province's health workforce shortages. Healthcare software firms willing to offer these technologies would therefore likely capture an important and immense market segment in the province. Quebec is working very hard to address issues, health and otherwise, regarding the demographic changes mentioned earlier, and has a 2005-2010 action plan for services to senior citizens who have lost autonomy, for example, which stresses community services, the only it believes to best provide all senior citizens who have lost autonomy. It intends to implement the program regionally through agencies in 2005/06, and has allocated $50 million for implementing the 2005-2010 Action and the 2005-2010 Mental Health Action Plans, both no doubt with likely significant healthcare software and ICT involvement. Quebec is also in the process of reforming its primary care services, and in December 2003, adopted the Local Health and Social Services Networks Act, which gave agencies the task of establishing a new way of organizing the services in each region, based on local service networks, 95 created province-wide in June 2004, to improve services accessibility, coordination, and continuity. A novel entity, the "centre de santé et de services sociaux" (CSSS), is the hub of each network, created from the amalgamation of local community service centers, long-term care centers, and shelters, and in most cases, a hospital. The central idea of the networks involves the multiplicity of health and social services providers to a local population being collectively responsible for the population. Thus, the network develops and executes initiatives to improve the health of the

149

entire population, public health activities, including health promotion and disease prevention, and, ensures improvement of access, continuity and quality of services, particularly for more vulnerable. These vulnerable groups include seniors that have lost autonomy, the mentally ill, persons with chronic diseases, at-risk youths, and individuals that need palliative care. The province wants the networks to have a hierarchy of services to guarantee enhanced complementarity between first-line, second-line, and third-line services via a common referral system between doctors.

It is clear that software developers interested in the healthcare software market in Quebec need to pay attention to these reforms to be able to identify potential avenues for product and service development to serve it effectively. There is also no doubt about the likely role that software and healthcare ICT in general would play in ensuring that these networks function optimally, as for one, communication and information sharing among the components of these networks would determine if in fact they function at all. Nonetheless, software firms, which could choose between vertical and horizontal markets, potential business opportunities huge in either, still need to do their homework, to understudy the market or as previously suggested outsource the task. Quebec has a variety of other programs that require significant healthcare software and ICT input, for example, its family medicine groups (FMG), of which it has now, 104, 71, from private clinic doctor groups, 17 accredited in public institutions, another 17, mixed, comprising private clinic groups and public healthcare facilities. Indeed, it intends based on the Ministère de la Santé et des Services Sociaux's 2005-2010 strategic plan, to form 300 FMGs, the goal, to have at least 70% of its peoples registered with a family doctor. Does this not indicate the important requirement for communication among these doctors, who according to the plan would provide home visits, among other health services, for example, when patients change doctors, or locations, among others? Would healthcare software firms not benefit from considering the technologies to offer both the patients and their doctors, for examples, to ease consultation, appointments, and billings, and even counseling, treatment, hotlines, and management monitoring, and via a variety of media for examples, mobile phones, or the Internet? Would patients for example, not be willing to purchase software, perhaps on their mobile phones that could enable them see their doctors while speaking with him or her on an important health issue on the go, and vice versa? The possibilities for software firms in the health sector are literally endless, the ability of the firm to discover the opportunities, perhaps the most significant obstacle standing between it and holding sway in a potentially huge market. This again, underscores the importance of process cycle analysis, and the need for these firms to embrace it. The province also has developed, in a collaborative effort by a number of agencies and professional groups, what it calls Network Clinics, a medical model aimed specifically to meet the challenges the characteristics of medical practice in urban centers pose, and the need for providing its peoples access to more inclusive healthcare during extended hours. These clinics enable access to medical services without an appointment outside a hospital ER daily 24/7, and coordinate operations between the doctors in a specific territory who look after the medical requirements of their clients, and the Centre de santé et de services sociaux (CSSS), thereby assuring access to and continuity of health and social services. These roles again, point to a significant role for healthcare software and ICT, in particular as the Network Clinic, which could be one clinic, a group of clinics, an FMG, or a family medicine unit that serves 50,000 people would need to communicate effectively to function efficiently and effectively. Furthermore, the network clinic provides access to comprehensive front-line medical services, including consultations with or without appointments, provision of essential emergency diagnostic services such as lab, x-rays and ultrasound on its own or in collaboration with other centers, and of medical monitoring services outside business hours for vulnerable clients by guaranteeing 24/7 access to a doctor, among others. These expected functions of the clinics also confirm the important role that healthcare ICT would play in their operations and the need for software firms keen on entering this market to appreciate fully their primary elements and the issues that are crucial to their success. Part of what we have been doing in our discussion is akin to the process cycle analysis that we advocate. It is a purely discovery process that could yield substantial dividend, and outweigh the efforts involved in conducting a successful analysis. So much is happening in the health sector and so many determinants and drivers of health services provision that knowing how much a province or territory plans to spend on healthcare software, and other ICT is not enough to take strategic decisions regarding product and service developments. Such decisions would be more meaningful were the software firm to understand the issues underlying the budget allocation, if the issues were short-term or enduring, if they were localized or applicable to the entire province or territory, and many such issues, an understanding that a thorough process cycle analysis would give. As with the provinces discussed so far, Nova Scotia, and indeed, all the other provinces and territories in Canada are investing in healthcare software and other ICT for reasons common to them all, for example, to meet the ideals of Medicare, but also to do so simultaneously curtailing the ever-increasing healthcare costs. In an April 18, 2006 press release by the Ministry of Health in Nova Scotia, Premier Rodney MacDonald revealed that the Department of Health is investing over C$10 million in a new digital diagnostic system at hospitals across the province, which would enable allow physicians and their patients to make faster and better treatment decisions. The new equipment is a component of a project, the Picture Archive, and Communications System (PACS) expansion project, already implemented in every district health Authority, to replace almost all film-based imaging in the province with faster, safer, and more streamlined processes, in effect to improve access to and the quality of healthcare delivery in the province. "Our plan is to introduce new information technology across the province that will improve the quality of care and access to tests and treatment," Premier Rodney MacDonald noted. He added, "The PACS system, which is part of this plan, will mean quicker treatment decisions and the reduction of unnecessary travel for many patients." According to the health Minister, "This technology helps reduce the time a patient has to wait...We are allowing doctors to spend more time with their patients and are providing Nova Scotians with health-care services as close to home as possible." Clearly, software firms interested in doing business in this province would want to know the status of the use in hospitals in the province, of digital technology for digital image capture, storage and transmission, and which hospital is using this technology for what, for examples, X-rays, or CT scans, or ultrasounds, or MRIs, or in fact for all. It also should want to know the firms in the market that it would be competing with, and the improvement that it could make on the products and services that they offer, again, underscoring the need for process cycle analysis. There is no doubt about the potential market opportunities for software for information and digital image management, for example in this province, and the analyses would likely reveal the other markets that might not in fact be immediately obvious. While some firms are already involved in the project, there are also likely to be worthwhile business opportunities in both the vertical, and horizontal markets for other software firms as doctors and other healthcare professionals for example, GPs would need the appropriate software to receive the transmitted digital images. The PACS expansion project is a partnership between the Health districts in Nova Scotia, the Department of Health, and Canada Health Infoway, the President and CEO, of which latter, Richard Alvarez, noted, "Nova Scotia is providing health-care professionals with faster access to better information by using diagnostic imaging, a key component of the electronic health record". He added, "This will go a long way towards improving the efficiency, accessibility, and quality of patient care in Canada's health-care system." The project started in 2004, costs, $25 million, Canada Health Infoway, contributing $12 million, the rest, $3 million, expected from the federal medical equipment fund. The province is also investing on other healthcare ICT initiatives and would likely continue to invest even more to achieve its healthcare delivery objectives in the short and long terms. Indeed, the province now has its hospital information system implemented in 34 hospitals across eight district health authorities, facilitating access to patient information by healthcare providers. On March 30, 2006, Health Minister Chris d'Entremont announced that connecting the eight districts completed one of the most detailed hospital information-system implementations in the country. The project's completion was an important step towards creation of an electronic health record (EHR) in the province, prior to which over 70% of the province's health-care facilities lacked the appropriate information systems to confront patient management conundrums, easy access to patient information with the new system, no doubt going to improve the quality of healthcare delivery in the province. Thus, the new system makes it unnecessary for patients to repeat the same medical history several times, has reduced wait times for test results and X-rays, and cut down on duplicated tests and procedures, saving time and money. It also provides better information about the quality and access to services, thereby assisting in health services planning, for example by facilitating more precise tracking of wait times data, which offers valuable information for resource allocation and utilization. Noted Mr. d'Entremont, "This system is an investment that will enable us to manage our health-care system more effectively now and in the future," an investment initiated by the provincial government in March 2001 at a total cost of $55.7 million. That the hospital information system is a crucial part of the province's all-encompassing health-information management strategy, which includes electronic health records, indicates the likelihood of continued investments in these and other relevant health information and communication technologies by this province in the near future, with corresponding major business openings for software firms. The examples we have given so far represent the pattern of significant investments in healthcare software and healthcare ICT across Canada. There is therefore no doubt that we would discover innumerable projects past, ongoing and planned if we considered each province and territory in our discussion. Suffice to emphasize, as we have all along, that for software firms to exploit the healthcare software markets, they ought to know the markets and to appreciate the reasons opportunities exist in them. They also should realize that current opportunities could trigger others, and understand whether market opportunities are enduring or fleeting, among other important information that could help the firms in planning product and service developments for those markets that interest them. Such exercises, which we termed process cycle analyses in our discussion are sine qua non for success in Canadian healthcare software, and indeed, in the entire healthcare ICT markets.

References:

1. Sigrid Schirdewahn S. Public Speaking: How Canadians view the roles of ICTs in the health sector. Office of Health and the Information Highway, Health Canada. In *Healthcare Information Management & Communications Canada*, Vol. XVI, No.3, 3rd Quarter, October 2002. Available at: http://www.hc-sc.gc.ca/hcs-sss/pubs/ehealth-esante/2002-publi-opin-speak/index_e.html Accessed on August 14, 2006

2. Silversides, A. Pharmacies receiving massive rebates from generic drug-makers. *CMAJ* August 15, 2006; 175 (4). Available at: http://www.cmaj.ca/cgi/content/full/175/4/342 Accessed on August 14, 2006

3. Priest, Alicia. Alberta pharmacists may get prescribing powers. CMAJ 2006 175 (5): p. 463

4. Available at: http://www.health.gov.on.ca/transformation/information/information_mn.html Accessed on August 19, 2006

5. Available at: http://www.health.gov.on.ca/transformation/providers/information/ses_report/ses_erie_stc.pdf Accessed on August 19, 2006

6. Dunlop S, Coyte P, McIsaac W. Socioeconomic status and the utilization of physician's services: Results from the Canadian National Population Health Survey. *Social Science and Medicine*. 2000; 51:123-33.

7. Health Canada. The population health template: Key elements and actions that define a population health approach. Strategic Policy Directorate of the population and Public Health Branch. July 2001.

8. Frolich N, Mustard C. A regional comparison of socio-economic and health indices in a Canadian province. *Social Science and Medicine*. 1996; 42 (9):1273-81

9. Health Information Partnership, Eastern Ontario Region. Census 2001 profile of Eastern Ontario: Index of relative socio-economic disadvantage. Kingston, Ontario; 2005.

10. Public Health Agency of Canada. Population health approach - The determinants of health. Ottawa. 1997.

11. Lipman EL, Boyle MH, Dooley MD, Offord DR. Child well-being in single-mother families. *Journal of the American Academy of Child and Adolescent Psychiatry*. 2002; 41(1):75-82.

12. Wilson K, Rosenberg MW. Exploring the determinants of health for First Nations peoples in Canada: can existing frameworks accommodate traditional activities? *Social Science and Medicine*. 2002; 55:2017-31

13. Picot G, Hou F. The rise in low-income rates among immigrants in Canada. Ottawa: Statistics Canada; 2003. Analytical Studies Branch research paper. Catalogue No. 11F0019MIE No. 198.

14. Available at:

http://www.health.gov.on.ca/transformation/providers/information/current_state.pdf Accessed on August 19, 2006

15. Available at:
http://www.health.gov.on.ca/transformation/providers/information/future_st
ate.pdf Accessed on August 19, 2006

16. Available at:
http://www.health.gov.on.ca/english/media/news_releases/archives/nr_06/j
ul/nr_071206_2.html Accessed on August 19, 2006

17. Available at: http://www.healthcareitnews.com/printStory.cms?id=5357
Accessed on August 20, 2006

18. Available at: http://www.hc-sc.gc.ca/hcs-sss/pubs/hisp-psis/telehealth-
infrastructure/index_e.html Accessed on August 20, 2006

19. Available at:
http://pdfdl.oceighty.net/pdf2html.php?url=http://www.health.gov.sk.ca/mc
_dp_shin_ar_2004-05.pdf Accessed on August 20, 2006

20. Available at:
http://www.cbc.ca/story/canada/national/2005/06/09/newscoc-
health050609.html Accessed on August 20, 2006

21. Available at:
http://publications.msss.gouv.qc.ca/acrobat/f/documentation/2005/05-
7... (PDF) *(238.9) kb* Accessed on August 20, 2006

Driver-Dynamics and Healthcare Software Business in Canada

The Canadian health scene is truly changing and fast. Issues ranging from funding model to soaring health spending are generating intense debates, policy reforms, and interests by the public. Developments in global health are adding to the mix, necessitating intersectoral collaborative efforts within the country, and between it and others. Demographic changes, the prevalence and patterns of diseases, known and emerging and the evolution of knowledge in a variety of domains including health, management, and technology, is inspiring a paradigm shift in healthcare delivery. With a new process developed by University of Arkansas researchers for example, resulting in three-dimensional nanomaterial, specifically paper, made of pulp from titanium oxide nanowires, it is not far-fetched to conjecture the emergence perhaps in the not-too-distant future, of inexpensive nano-antibiotics, analgesics, and other pharmaceuticals, the researchers having shown the material's use as a low-cost nontoxic photocatalyst. The paper being a photocatalyst could regenerate its chemical composition after exposure to light, for example, erasing the content written on it, a capability, perhaps induced chemically or by other catalytic processes, applied to these nano-medications that could it result in their recycling, the cost saving potential no doubt enormous. Indeed, the emergence of new, targeted drug delivery systems (DDS) that integrate pharmaceutical and polymer science, molecular biology, information science, and bioconjugate chemistry would in the near future have significant impact on the software and healthcare ICT industry.

This is inevitable as we strive for tighter control of systems biorecognition, pharmacokinetics, pharmacodynamics, immunogenicity and toxicity, among others, in our overall efforts to achieve the dual healthcare delivery goals of qualitative service delivery simultaneously reducing costs. Consider also the recent development by computers scientists in Scotland of software program for children that require computerized speech aids, the computer program able to generate jokes, which by making it possible for non-speaking children to utilize puns and other yarns, assist them in developing their language and communication skills[1]. University of Dundee researchers developed the System to Augment Non-speakers Dialogue Using Puns (Standup) project. Children using the software choose a word or compound word from the system's dictionary that will form part or all of the punch line, the software thereafter writing the joke's opener. The program compares the selected word with other words in its dictionary for phonetic likeness or concepts that connect the words. It then allots them to a pun template. There is no doubt that this software, which demonstrates the breadth of the scope for health software, most untapped, in Canada, and indeed, worldwide, could help many children who are unable to speak, considering the beneficial effect of language play, including use of humor, on a child's language and communication skills development. The market opportunities for such software in Canada, for example in children's hospitals, and other health resources for the management of children with autism for example, and those with developmental delays, and even in schools, regular and special, would likely be significant, particular judging by the positive response to the software by children during trials. Researchers noted that it boosted the confidence of the children, and their language skills, and enabled them to control conversations and to amuse other people, also buoying their self-esteem. The researchers are in fact negotiating with manufacturers to integrate the software into computerized-speech aids for children, in effect, the development of this software, opening another potential value chain, which could perhaps open yet another, in a continuous process of value creation, with the potential for significant revenue generation, a process for which Canadian software firms should always be ready. Incidentally, and in keeping with not just the magnitude of the health sector market potential, its payers' increasing awareness of the multidimensional value of healthcare ICT, hence increased investments in these technologies but also on the increasing competitiveness among software vendors in the sector, the need for re-conceptualizing the value chain is rife. In other words, for healthcare software and healthcare ICT firms, the value chain should not just be modal, a cascade of activities in a stepwise progression towards value creation, but rather should be flexible and multimodal, the firm seeking value actively in vertical and horizontal, indeed multiple directions, capitalizing on the chances its core competence offers for such multimodal forays. Let us consider some examples from the mental health field. There is research evidence for examples for the proven benefits of psychotherapy in several psychiatric disorders such as bipolar disorder[2], and for those of cognitive therapy (CT), cognitive-behavioral therapy (CBT), and interpersonal psychotherapy (IPT) for depression[3]. In fact, cognitive therapy and antidepressants are just as effective for the initial treatment of severe depression, but the enduring effect of the former may be more cost-effective, long-term[4], findings from a recent study showing that over the 16-month study, antidepressant treatment cost \$2590 on average versus \$2250 for cognitive therapy, the difference even more in time[4]. The use of software and other healthcare ICT such the Internet, telephone, videoconference, even email and text messaging, among others, to deliver these psychotherapies, in particular, cognitive, and cognitive behavior therapies is gaining currency[5,6,7]. Psychoeducation, which is more than simply providing information to patients on diseases and health matters but also includes a more complex mix of multimedia tools and other approaches to improve functional outcomes for the ill and their families is also proven effective, resulting in not just clinical improvement, fewer illness relapses, but also cost savings, fewer

161

hospitalizations[8]. By improving treatment compliance, for example, structured psychoeducation as opposed to unstructured group therapy sessions could enhance treatment efficacy, a recent study reporting more stable lithium levels during psychoeducation for patients with bipolar disorder[9], thereby reducing morbidity, and saving costs. Another noteworthy example is the issue of overweight/obesity, particularly considering findings from a recent Canadian Medical Association (CMA) commissioned Ipso-Reid telephone survey of parents in June/July 2006[10], which showed parents tend to gloss over the weight problems of their children. Thus, 26% of Canadian children aged 2-17 are obese/overweight, but just 9% of Canadian parents thought their own children were. However, despite being apparently unwilling to admit the health status of their own children, many parents endorsed proposals aimed at improving children's health, such as dietary and physical activity measures, which makes another recent research finding that computer-automated behavioral counseling could enhance weight loss, indeed, efficiently cost-effectively, of potential market significance for healthcare software firms[11]. Researchers at the University of North Carolina at Chapel Hill and the Miriam Hospital in Providence, R.I., reported the significant weight loss by persons enrolled in an Internet-based e-counseling weight loss program in a study published in the Aug. 14, 2006 issue of the Archives of Internal Medicine. Indeed, earlier studies by the research team also found that Internet weight loss programs are more effective when they include e-mail counseling that an expert provides, the researchers noting that automating such counseling would make it available to many more individuals at a fraction of the cost of more intensive treatment programs. According to co-author Dr. Rena Wing, director of the Weight Management and Diabetes Research Center at The Miriam Hospital and Brown Medical School "Compared to e-mail counseling provided by a human, a computer pre-programmed with messages based on specific criteria is a highly efficient treatment approach that can be more widely disseminated among the population in need." No doubt, such programs, refined and modifiable to meet individual needs have immense potential market value in Canada, and it does in the U.S., and indeed elsewhere, considering the ubiquity of the Internet worldwide. These examples represent the variety of developments in different health domains that offer potential market opportunities for software firms. There are also developments in non-health domains that influence those in the health domains and vice versa. The nature and momentum of these developments should be of interest to software firms as they are likely to affect the interplay of health and non-health related factors in the outcome of efforts at healthcare policy formulation and delivery, hence of the type and extent of investments, capital or otherwise in the health sector. The healthcare software industry, being a major player in this dynamics, would indeed, have to be aware of the issues surrounding the interaction of these factors at various levels, such as administrative, functional, and funding, among others. The intensity of the competition in the industry makes this imperative for any software firm seeking to do business in the health sector to survive, let alone thrive. The market openings in the various health jurisdictions in the country for example are doubtless, huge, and require software firms to appreciate fully the issues relevant to their markets of interest within a province or territory, and even in a health jurisdiction within such entities. The scale and diversity of such issues, both health and non-health related are undeniably massive, which underscores the need for focus on strategic intent, and this does not need to target a firm's competition, but could be self-benchmarked. It does not also preclude flexibility, but rather embraces it, considering that such focus could reveal opportunities hitherto cryptic, but the exploration of which the firm's core competence even if not an exact fit, is modifiable to, the benefits accruable from that exercise, albeit in the long term potentially far in excess of the resources invested in it. The key point though is that the firm is unlikely to make this "discovery" in an armchair, literally, as it would likely require putting much effort into exploring the issues mentioned earlier in process cycle analyses.

T hese ongoing decomposition/exposition cycles constitute the ingredients for

the full appreciation of known processes underlying the issues in question, and in ferreting those essentially subterranean. The following example of the recent deployment of an advanced healthcare information system-platform for a rehabilitation clinic clearly illustrates this point. The platform, a collaborative systems integration effort of several vendors such as TIMA, MedAppz, Cryptek, DP Solutions, HP, Juniper, and Olympus installed at the Universal Industrial Clinic (UIC), in the City of Newark, the clinic which specializes in delivering care to employees injured while at work, previously using an analog, or paper-based, data/information milieu[12]. UIC, on opting to migrate to a digital and paperless environment discovered that most electronic medical records vendors had major defects regarding, besides price, such issues as data/information security, data import/export, portability, scalability, and analytical/mining tools, hence did not essentially meet its needs, and led to the collaboration from which the MedAppz iSuite platform emerged. The platform will enable the integration of various platforms and hardware to offer IUC maximum flexibility yet not being overly complex. The platform would be able to deliver healthcare delivery processes such as billing, analytics, messaging, diagnostics, and transcription, and administrative processes such as appointment scheduling and document management, the developers emphasizing that it would increase rather than compromise data/information security as some other systems integration platforms that simply "bundle" multi third party platforms do. Process cycle analyses would thus, provide software firms the critical data and information, for examples that they need to appreciate wholly the data and information needs of different market players, for examples, doctors, nurses, hospital executives, hospital accountants, even the IT staff of health organizations, on the one hand, and the competition in their markets of interest, on the other. Consider PACS for example. Would it not be necessary for software firms to know for example that Philips Medical Systems recently signed a Preferred Solution Agreement with Canada Health Infoway for iSiteTM PACS, a solution for Diagnostic Imaging Repositories and Regional Web Viewing? Does this agreement not suggest the preference of Canada Infoway, which supports the bulk of the country's healthcare ICT projects for the Philips solution regarding standards? Should these software firms not therefore consider aligning their products and services with these standards? Indeed, Philips, based on the agreement, will assist clients in speeding up the implementation of standards that Canada Health Infoway support, and of a network of interoperable healthcare ICT solutions throughout the country. The agreement also offers health authorities in the country benchmarks for healthcare ICT acquisition via the company's exclusive Fee-per-Study Total Cost of Ownership (TCO) business model. The issue of standards is no doubt crucial to the success of the entire e-health efforts in Canada, and it applies not just to the operability of disparate software and healthcare ICT within the country, but also between it and others, as the announcement by Tony Clement, Minister of Health, and Xavier Bertrand, France's Minister of Health and Solidarity, indicated. The two Ministers signed a Joint Declaration of Intent, announced on August 15, 2006 that outlines mutual work the two countries intend to carry out in the next four years in major areas such as pandemic influenza preparedness and the strengthening of their health care systems[13]. In achieving their goals to share expertise and experience in these domains, it would be necessary for their health information systems to communicate, and indeed, for them to embrace novel software and other healthcare ICT that would enable them achieve those objectives, and either way, there would have to be agreements on standards. A key area of co-operation between the two countries as agreed in the Joint Declaration of Intent includes programs related to HIV/AIDS, sexually transmitted infections, hepatitis B/C, and tuberculosis and sexual and reproductive health, in particular as they concern vulnerable populations. Right there, the scale of the potential contribution of healthcare ICT to the actualization of these programs is evident. No doubt, these programs would cover all three disease-prevention levels, namely, primary, secondary, and tertiary prevention, creating immense opportunities for the development of relevant software and other healthcare ICT for marketing worldwide. As opportunities emerge would also likely challenges, and software firms must be ready for both, a surfeit of which the declaration would likely create. Specifically, the Joint Declaration of Intent will allow Canada and France to benefit from their experiences in ICT as they affect e-health and telehealth. Furthermore, the two countries will trade benchmarks in wait time management, access to medications, and human resource planning, and cooperate in areas such as physical activity, cancer, management of chronic diseases, in promoting mental health and in influenza pandemic preparedness and response. With regard to the latter, they agreed on their plans in both areas in support of the outcomes of the October 2005 Ottawa Statement on Global Pandemic Influenza Readiness, and in general, to collaborate on implementing in the two countries, the new WHO International Health Regulations, in whose revision Canada was instrumental. The regulations would assist countries globally address international public health emergencies, and it just about time we did, considering the increasing intercalated nature of our world, with new disease outbreaks in one part with the potential not just to affect another, but in fact the entirety of the rest. New viruses for example, emerge from time to time, as is recently the case with China reporting six cases of human bocavirus in children, the first infections in that country associated with the newly known virus[14], first reported in Sweden in September 2005, information about the infection and its root, sparse. There have also been cases of the virus in about 5% of mostly young pneumonia patients in rural Thailand, and in Japanese and Australian children with respiratory tract infections. With SARS outbreak in 2002-03, and concerns about an imminent bird flu pandemic and global preparedness or its lack to response to, not to mention, prevent it, many would likely have similar concerns regarding the human bocavirus, in particular regarding the potential consequences of its seeming ubiquity across the globe. No doubt, healthcare software and other healthcare ICT would be playing significant parts in measures to alleviate such concerns. In other words, the initiatives that would emanate from the objectives of the Canada/France alliance, including in addressing global health issues, would require heavy software and healthcare ICT input. Thus, the increased likelihood of both countries having to invest in these technologies in future as these initiatives emerge would offer Canadian software firms market opportunities but also sire challenges, inevitably. Issues concerning the Internet, broadband, and data retention, among others, exemplify the simultaneous potential for business opportunities and challenges that Canadian software firms ought to be prepared to confront in the health sector. Let us first consider the challenges, potential and real. Recently, broadband firm Qwest Communications International on August 22, 2006, robustly endorsed U.S. federal legislation requiring Internet providers to keep records of their customers' behavior, the first time a broadband provider has advocated such laws, and a step that many believe could speed efforts in Congress to pass new legislation[15]. Jennifer Mardosz, Qwest's corporate counsel and chief privacy officer reported praised efforts by politicians to force broadband providers to engage in "data retention", which some including the U.S. government argue would help in investigating terrorism and child exploitation among others, the conflict between balancing the interests of privacy and law enforcement, immediately obvious, regarding such laws. Even for Quest, which has a market capitalization of $16.5 billion and 784,000 wireless and 1.7 million DSL customers, guarded its clients' privacy rights, requiring the National Security Agency to obtain a court order to conduct electronic surveillance, in May 2006, and already keeps logs for over 99% of its services for one year, the stand seems curious. Privacy groups and many Internet providers have opposed mandatory data retention fervently, the U.S. Internet Industry

167

Association lambasting the approach of current proposals, and the Information Technology Association of America raising serious concerns about legislation. Controversy over the issue of data retention laws does not only rage in the U.S. On December 14, 2005, the European Parliament enacted a new data retention law that will require Internet service providers and phone companies to keep data on every phone call and e-message for between six months and two years, although there also, criticisms of the law being a threat to personal privacy also abound[16]. Telecommunications providers in Europe now have to keep data for example, time of call and its duration, for both cell phone and fixed line, regardless of the call answered or not, these and other details making it possible to track the caller. Regarding the Internet, they will need to keep information on the time of connection to the Internet, the individual's IP address, and details of e-mail messages and VoIP calls, but the communications' contents. While Qwest has issued a rebuttal of the news.com story denying advocating retention laws, its Chief Privacy Officer, Jennifer Mardosz, saying that she was speaking about Colorado State laws already in place[17], there is no doubt that these laws have significant implications for healthcare ICT diffusion, privacy and confidentiality being key issues hampering the widespread adoption of these technologies. Qwest in a statement insisted it does not believe there is a need for legislation but that firms should voluntarily retain records of Internet Protocol address assignments "to protect customer privacy and safeguard citizens from online predators[17]". Canadian privacy law indicates general requirements on data retention and obliteration, but not many patent legal duties on either. Laws such as Ontario's new Personal Health Information Protection Act offer reasonable privacy protection, but with the issue of data retention creating so much furor in some circles, broadband penetration increasing in many countries including Canada facilitating healthcare going increasingly online, the privacy of health data and information would likely feature prominently in this debate. This would likely pose a potential obstacle to market expansion for innovative healthcare software and other ICT for web-based service delivery. Besides privacy issues, Telcos and ISPs are also concerned about the storage costs implications of these laws, and the possible significant burden they would impose on the competitiveness on the global stage of the e-communications industry in jurisdictions where such laws are operational. This is not to mention the effects of the laws on the realization of collaborative efforts, for example that between Canada and France mentioned earlier. In addition, earlier in 2005, the European parliament passed a directive from the European Commission for ISPs and Telcos to keep data for six to 12 months, again in spite of rigorous protests by privacy advocates, again highlighting the potential breach of this information and the need for cutting-edge software security solutions to protect the data and information. The European laws billed to take effect in 2008, apply to a wide range of "traffic" and "location" data, for examples, the identities of the customers' exchanges, the date, time, and length of phone calls, VoIP calls or e-mail messages, and the device's location used for making the calls, but not the call's contents. Furthermore, ISPs allot IP addresses typically to clients from a pool depending on a computer's use then, via two customary methods, namely, Point-to-Point Protocol over Ethernet and the Dynamic Host Configuration Protocol, the law mandating them to report detected child pornography to the National Center for Missing and Exploited Children, which contacts the police. Software firms could aim to develop products and services for improving this detection or to address concerns about other technical and other issues. As noted for example, Kate Dean, director of the U.S. Internet Service Provider Association, whose members include AOL, AT&T, BellSouth, and EarthLink, "The proposal to store enormous amounts of data on subscribers and keep it live for a lengthy period of time raises serious technical, legal and security concerns". However, as privacy advocates argue, it does not matter whether the laws compel Internet providers to retain IP address records, or logs, or indeed, other records of Internet usage, since all would essentially amount to breaching individual privacy. Furthermore, any local or state law-enforcement official on the pretext of an investigation, for example, drug trafficking might gain access to private health information, they contend. The question then is whether it is technology, law, or an admixture of both, and in the latter case, to which extent of either, which would really protect patient's health records. Is it possible that some sophisticated software would emerge that could obviate the need for these laws, that could ensure the realization of the objectives of the laws, simultaneously protecting individual privacy? Would developing such software not be turning challenges into market opportunities? Should Canadian software firms not be seeking to develop such software and indeed other appropriate software to address the information privacy and security issues that hinder the widespread adoption of healthcare information and communication technologies in the health sector? The two commonest Internet access services are broadband or "high speed access" and narrowband, also known as "dial-up access", although revenues from broadband access continue to increase significantly more by 23% in 2004, for example, than from dial-up access, which actually fell by 19% during the same year, mostly due to Internet users migrating to the former. With more Canadians using the Internet for a variety of daily tasks including seeking health services, six out of ten Canadian households connected to the Internet in 2004, up from four out of 10 in 2000, with benefits to the Canadian ISP industry, revenues up by of 9% to $1.7 billion in the same year, addressing these issues is critical.

Another key driver in the health sector is the issue of hospital wait times.

Indeed, a recent survey conducted between July and August 2006, suggests that over a third of Canadian households feel that they did not have access to timely healthcare in the last three months, 37% actually according to the poll that

Decima Research conducted. The researchers asked 3,000 respondents whether someone in their home needed care, what kind of care, and if the felt they waited too long[18], the results indicating that about 75% of Canadian households needed some type of healthcare in the last three months, 50% of who reported that they could not receive it fast enough. The survey also showed that the most often required types of care were an appointment with a family doctor or a specialist, diagnostic tests, and emergency hospital treatment, access to all of which the deployment of the appropriate software could help improve, and which underscores why Canadian software firms need to conduct thorough process cycle analyses to understand their markets. Would such analyses not reveal the underlying processes involved with these activities, and would it not be possible therefore for software firms to appreciate better, for which processes to develop what software? Should Canadian software firms, at least those interested in the market, not actually be engaged in process cycle analyses for the entire wait times issue in the respective health jurisdiction of interest, as even though certain processes might be common to the issue across the country, there are likely to be local flavours to it? Incidentally, one such common process, that of information provision, as this example shows, is one area that software and other healthcare ICT firms could explore for potential market opportunities. According to a new report from the U.S., State health department Web sites are increasingly user-friendly over the past five years, but a significant number of these sites continue to be difficult to read, only presented in English and are not accessible to persons with disabilities[19]. According to researchers Darrell West, Ph.D., and Edward Alan Miller, Ph.D., of Brown University, "People in particular need of up-to-date and accurate health care information appear least able to share in the benefits of online government resources." The study, published in the latest issue of the Journal of Health Care for the Poor and Underserved observed that while 50% of Americans read at an eighth-grade level, only 20% of state health department Web sites were at that level in 2005, most written at a 10th- or 11th-grade level.

As West noted, "If official health Web sites are written at too high a level for visitors to comprehend, the technology revolution will not reach its full potential as a public health information tool." In 2005, only 42% of the state sites had standard features for examples, larger font options, and audio tags to facilitate access to them by individuals with physical impairments, features advocacy groups insist federal laws for example, the 1990 Americans with Disabilities Act, mandate, although they may not apply to State-managed web sites, as they do to those federal. Just 34% of state sites had medical information available in a language besides English in 2005 numbers West and Miller insisted would be unacceptable under federal election and education statutes, standards, which if applied to may states, would be unmet based on the findings of this study. These issues no doubt apply to Canada, where access to current and accurate health information is important in solving at least in part, the "wait times" issue. Indeed, it is also important in rectifying in a general sense, the issue of the pervasive information asymmetry in the health sector, a key hindrance to the achievement by the country's health system of the dual healthcare delivery goals of qualitative health services provision simultaneously reducing health spending. With the increasing emphasis on customer-driven healthcare delivery, would even private healthcare web sites, and indeed, all websites for that matter not need to meet accessibility standards similar to those mentioned above, and could software firms not help in achieving this goal, generating significant revenues from the market openings in the process? The study also noted the improvement in privacy and security policies among state sites since 2000, due partly to the 1996 federal health privacy act termed HIPAA, as only 8% of state health department Web sites had an online privacy policy in 2000 versus 86% in 2005. However, it also noted the variations in accessibility and privacy policies, among states, web sites from Southern states, for examples the most readable and most likely to offer those with disabilities adequate access, whereas sites from Western states are most likely to offer non-English materials. Such variations would likely also occur in Canada between provinces, and even within health jurisdictions in the same province. This again, highlights the need for software firms interested in this market to appreciate fully the issues involved to be best able to offer the right products and services to address the market's Internet accessibility, privacy, and security concerns. Some provinces and territories might be interested in upgrading their websites and in fact, other aspects of their health information systems, simultaneously for a number of technical reasons besides harmonizing the technologies involved with information privacy and security, among others. Some of these projects might be sufficiently large to warrant the collaboration of a number of different software firms, and others might create opportunities for friendly or hostile acquisition for software firms, the events occurring at this technical front, sometimes becoming key drivers of events in both the health and healthcare ICT industries, as the example of Isoft shows. This firm is at the core presently of the U.K National Health Service's multi-billion- pound IT upgrade program, BT and CSC, the American computer giant, both reportedly potential bidders for the firm, despite that both have significant IT contracts with the NHS, to which Isoft is a major supplier[20]. Isoft is the software subcontractor in three of the five regional organizational "clusters" for the IT upgrade, and it even garnered an important extra supply deal with CSC only the week before in mid-August 2006. However, Connecting for Health, the agency that oversees the NHS program, reportedly might not favor the anticipated takeover because its is not so keen on the concept of a reduction in the number of suppliers to the program, or in vertical amalgamation of its prime contractors and their suppliers, more so involving a major player such as Isoft. Meantime Isoft has negotiated new extra funding from its bankers, made public on August 25, 2006 when Isoft released delayed results including a major goodwill writedown that took it to a £343m pre-tax loss, rather than have its shares shelved. Now, the firm admitted accounting irregularities, the subject of a Financial Services Authority (FSA) investigation over potentially misleading statements to the market. The interplay of this investigation, the potential acquisition mentioned earlier, and Accenture, another leading player in the NHS IT scheme being in contract renegotiation talks, the firm the major contractor for the east/northeast NHS regions, and has earmarked £250m against losses on the contracts, among other factors are critical to the extent of the delay in the program. The magnitude of this delay, and its inevitable costs overruns, will likely determine the pace of additional healthcare ICT investments in the country, and of course of the realization of the benefits of these technologies on the health system, which it could further compromise by heightening the opposition including among healthcare professionals to several aspects of the IT program. Accenture for example, some sources noted, had thought about leaving the program, but that talks were ongoing with Connecting for Health, a withdrawal that would potentially be devastating for the £6.2 billion IT program, a program previously criticized severely for delays and cost overruns. Thus, Canadian software firms need to be cognizant of the potential interplay of various health and non-health factors in the evolution of events that could have potential significance for their markets of interests. As noted earlier, the increasing focus on the healthcare client, hence their needs, including for accessibility to health services, underlines the key role that information provision, and by extension, knowledge management would play in the future of healthcare delivery in Canada. Considering the interests of most people in their health, these issues are likely to be also of more interests to healthcare software firms as they realize their market potential. Consider a recent survey of seniors for example that showed that they worry more about health than money[21]. Almost 70% of seniors 65 years and older care said that they care more about their health and well-being than about their finances, according to the report that SecureHorizons conducted on 750 seniors in 10 different markets, including Tampa, Florida, about their worries as they become older. Tampa seniors ranked personal finances, spirituality, mental health, and being able to care for themselves, after health, in importance in descending order. At the national level, health, and well-being were first, spirituality, self-care, mental health, and personal finances, next in descending order of importance. Additionally, the telephone survey showed that 80% of seniors said that they keep current on the latest health news, physicians 43% the most popular source of health information for seniors, which exemplifies the information asymmetry mentioned earlier, and is a relic of the paternalistic traditions of the medical profession. The Internet 25% is the next commonest resource seniors consult, younger respondents likelier to seek health information online than older ones, again significant for the increasing trend toward Internet use for health information search and the potential for market opening for healthcare software firms. This likely applies to Canada, which also has an essentially aging population with identical demographic, health, and socio-economic characteristics with those in the U.S. The survey also showed that concern about end of life planning is higher than the national average in Tampa, with 47% of those surveyed expressing concern, versus 38% nationally, maintaining physical independence and mobility, a key concern for Tampa seniors, among concerns regarding health and well-being, highlighting the potential markets for assistive software and other technologies. Availability of affordable prescription drugs and finding ways to stay healthy, were second and third concerns respectively, among health and well-being concerns, again, both pointers to potential healthcare software markets, and indicative of the need for further process cycle analyses in health jurisdictions of interest in Canada by its software firms to assist in strategic product and service developments. These examples show the eclectic nature of the factors that operate in tandem to determine the direction of not just health services provision in Canada, but also that of healthcare software and ICT investments, and of the markets for these technologies, both vertical and horizontal. Some of these factors are static, for example, the geographic locations of towns and cities in the country, others dynamic, for example, the changing population structures in these towns and cities, including the ratio of the different age groups, gender, and even of the immigrant populations that they have. Some of the factors are health, others, not health-related. The interactions between some are simple and direct, for example, the likelier need for more health services the higher the population, and others complex, for example, the effect of technology standards on systems interoperability, and the lack thereof, on the disjointedness of systems even when functional, compromising the ability to reap the full healthcare delivery benefits of implemented systems. These differences regardless, it is up to the software firm keen to exploit existing markets, perhaps discover new ones to take the issue of engaging in thorough process cycle analyses, seriously, and if lacking in the human and other resources so to do, outsource the exercises.

W ould any healthcare software firm for example not want to be cognizant of

recent developments in the public versus private health issue in Canada such as the position of the Canadian medical Association on the issue? On August 23, 2006, Canadian doctor-delegates to the Canadian Medical Association policy conference in Charlottetown agreed that creating a parallel private system should remain an option but, minutes later, rejected the idea of allowing private insurance that would enable a parallel health system. The doctors also adopted a motion that the CMA should "acknowledge the strengths of Canada's publicly-funded healthcare system" and determine reforms to improve it, and that governments ought to lift the prohibition on doctors practicing in both the private and public system and that all doctors should be able to leave the public system, although discourage an exodus[22]. The passion with which the debate over private versus public health care unfolds in Canada is not in doubt, in particular since the Supreme Court decision in 2005 to enable residents of

Quebec access to private healthcare if they wished, and the moves the province has made subsequently toward effecting the decision of the highest court in the land. Many see the contest for the Presidency of the CMA, which also played out in Charlottetown, as a face-off between supporters of either of these two health systems, a highpoint in the history of an association that has supported the concept of publicly funded health care for a quarter of a century. Observers agree that the CMA came out of its meeting still essentially divided on the issue, and as its immediate past president, Dr. Collins-Nakai noted "So you might wonder what is the message that delegates delivered today?. Well, to be frank, it was mixed...But what delegates did say is that they don't want to close the door on any potential solution to improve access to our patients... (This is) a reflection of the level of frustration the physicians of Canada are feeling on behalf of their patients." Incidentally, Dr Brian Day, CMA President-elect, who assumes office in 2007, reportedly owns Canada's largest private healthcare clinic, and said at Charlottetown that "Like most Canadians and physicians, I believe there is a place for the private sector and for public and private partnerships," although insisted he would not use his position to promote private healthcare. The developments at the CMA meeting have important implications for healthcare delivery in the country. With the association comprising the primary healthcare providers that would use software and healthcare ICT aimed to improve clinical practice, and who directly or otherwise would be part of the use of a variety of other software not directly developed for but contributing to the exercise, their position on health services funding and related issues is crucial. For example, would we see, assuming that private healthcare delivery becomes entrenched in the country, a mass movement of doctors out of the public health system? If this happened, what implications would it have for the sustainability of the public health system, and could it mean the merging, or perhaps even closure of some services and hospital facilities, and what would this mean for the healthcare software industry in terms of up-and down-stream, vertical markets' opportunities? Would the public health system need innovative software and healthcare ICT to help deliver novel value propositions that make it economically viable, if for example, its clients also move en-masse to patronize the private health sector, at least those of them that could afford it? Could such shift in patient population to the private health sector leave some Canadians, who could not afford private healthcare with no or limited access to health services as public health services shut down or merge? Could software and other healthcare ICT help prevent this scenario by helping maintain affordable public health services for the depleted patrons of Medicare? These and many more questions would perhaps arise if and when a parallel private health system takes hold in Canada, and the answers to these questions would be crucial drivers of the future of health service provision and the role of healthcare software and other ICT in this regard. Here again, it is prudent for software firms to explore these questions and the issues that they raise, along with their processes to be able to appreciate fully, the markets current and future, hence be better prepared for the opportunities and challenges to expect from them. Conducting process cycle analyses is one sure way to reveal these issues and processes, and to be in a position to gain market edge, and to ensure that it derives return on its investments (ROI) developing inventive products and services for these markets. The scope and nature of these analyses would certainly vary with the generic interests of the software firm, as these could change with the discovery of new and profitable business avenues during the decomposition/exposition exercises. In other words, software firms should maintain a certain flexibility and agility in responding to the ever-shifting terrain of prospects and challenges that the health sector offers. To illustrate this point, consider the possibilities besides those mentioned above in the event of the emergence of large-scale, commercial, private sector involvement of health service provision in the country. In fact, the competition between the public and the private sector would just be one part of a critical dyadic of possibly even what we could term hyper-competition, as players in the private sector also jostle for clients amongst themselves. In the context of a client-focused healthcare delivery approach, this competition for clients would be even more intense. Private healthcare providers would need to offer products and services that would differentiate them from their competition in other to thrive, let alone prosper. We would then see various combinations of value propositions that could create immense market opportunities for healthcare software firms, as healthcare providers attempt to outperform one another using cutting-edge health information and communication technologies to deliver services at the primary, secondary and tertiary levels. Thus, the traditional family physician would transform itself via these technologies into a modern-day, healthcare delivery impresario, offering services that range from disease prevention to health promotion, and to treatment and rehabilitation services, depending on a variety of factors. We would also likely see the emergence of the "centers of excellence", highly specialized clinics and hospitals for the delivery of specific services for example, obstetric or cancer treatment services. Software firms with the right information, gleaned from the results of their process cycle analyses for example, would be better able to work with healthcare providers in designing and building software tailored to the providers' needs. They would also be able to develop and offer products and services independently to vertical and horizontal markets based on their appreciation of the needs of these markets. On the one hand consequent upon these developments would be the tendency of the software to become commoditized but on the other would be the energized creative impulse turned loose by the challenges of designing and developing customized software for health service providers and for specific population groups, for example seniors with chronic medical illnesses. Software firms would be able to develop for example, software that would not just enable or facilitate action, but would be constitutive, an "embedded" part of the healthcare provider's health information systems, working seamlessly with the others to ensure the smooth operations of

179

the entire systems complex. Such systems, much like the MedAppz iSuite platform discussed earlier, together perhaps even detecting and solving technical problems that arise, in a decidedly self-healing way. Thus, software firms would have the opportunity to be even more creative than before as they explore in detail the market openings that competition between the public and the private sector on the one hand, and between elements within the private sector on the other would engender with the latter becoming established, if indeed it did, in the country. As the healthcare consumer becomes increasingly discerning, would the competition intensify. Incidentally, not just the public that would become more discerning about health services delivery. Healthcare professionals also would as their professional reputation and progress depend ever more on their performance, which healthcare software and other ICT appropriately deployed, could help improve. However, the immediate problem regarding these technology end-users is to encourage them to use these technologies, particularly those of them in the health professions. In other words, change management software and services would increasingly be in demand in the Canadian health sector, as health establishments attempt to ensure that the healthcare ICT on which they invested substantially do not lie idle, shunned by the end-user. This would not be a one-off as such exercises would be necessary with the implementation and perhaps even upgrades of the technologies as the following example shows. A Royal College of Nursing (RCN) survey published on August 23, 2006 showed that the nurses' favorable opinion of the U.K's NHS IT developments is changing[23]. The largest ever survey of nurses' attitudes to IT and information issues, it revealed that nurses still feel overlooked regarding NHS IT decision making, indicates that they receive little training on utilizing IT and information, and that they expend great effort to access a PC at work, all essential components of the change management programs software firms may offer. The survey involved more than four thousand nurses from all over the UK. The results showed that 87% of nurses thought it was important that the authorities consulted them about IT plans and just 12% indicated they had adequate consultation, 38% that they had adequate information about current NHS IT developments, and 61% that they did not, including 26% who had no information whatsoever. Another area of concern according to the study was the dearth of training for nurses, 95% of participants indicating that nurse training was vital to the proposed electronic health record (EHR) system, succeeding, although 69% had not received any IT training at work in the last six months. The study noted no progress in this regard versus the results of past RCN surveys, and that this failure to involve and engage nurses explains if only in part, nurses' attitudes towards current NHS IT projects, underlining the importance of change management in healthcare software deployment. The study noted further that about 50% of nurses still believe they will improve their working lives, a 10% and 7% fall since 2004, and 2005, respectively, the percentage of nurses that that believed ICT developments would improve clinical care in 2004, 70%, also falling to 56% in 2006. Additionally, 40% of participants thought the ICT developments are good use of NHS funds, 43% did not, versus 21% in 2004, and just 11% in 2005. According to Dr Beverly Malone, RCN General Secretary, "In the current financial crisis in the NHS it is hardly surprising that nurses are expressing reservations about the large and expensive national NHS IT program. Nurses will be by far the largest group of health professionals using NHS IT systems, yet they are hardly being consulted, or informed, about developments." She added, "We know from experience that if front-line staff are not involved in change, it fails. This survey is the final wake up call for the government. They need to work much harder and, as a matter of urgency, ensure nurses are involved in the development and evaluation of IT program. Nurses are willing to work with the government on this, but we're not sure the government is willing to work with us." How right, and suggestive of the likely increased demand for healthcare software and other healthcare ICT not just in the U.K markets, but also in Canada, as these problems are hardly peculiar to the U.K., and as we noted earlier, as change management will likely be a continuous process, in particular with major software and healthcare ICT upgrades. As Sharon Levy Informatics advisor at the RCN, observed, "This is not just about teaching nurses to press buttons on a computer. Information and its use and management are central to nursing and delivering good patient care. We have got to give nurses the right training and support so that NHS and patients see the benefits that IT could bring to healthcare. If nurses continue to be ignored, a huge amount of money and effort could be wasted in yet another failed public sector IT program." There is no doubt about the truism of this observation, which is starting to receive serious attention by healthcare policy makers and which would mean increasing interests and investments in change management technologies and services in the near future.

Considering the very nature of the country's health system, with the provinces and territories essentially running health services provision, much of the direction of the public health system would depend on how the executives and boards of hospitals and health jurisdictions in the country perceive and conduct health policy. As noted above, factors such as the attitude of nurses and other healthcare professionals to healthcare ICT projects would influence their investments in certain healthcare ICT-related products and services, but would also influence their approaches to managing these technologies vis-à-vis their information requirements. They would increasingly need software for example that could make it easier for them to manipulate and analyze trend data and information in clinical and non-clinical domains alike, for examples population health indices and complex financial management data, respectively. For administrative and management processes, data for examples, multi-level budgetary variance and allocation data, resource use and optimization data, and data and information on trends within the establishment would be critical to crunch and organize into actionable information and knowledge, markets for software that could help achieve these goals likely to be in great demand. This is more so, considering what some would term the frenetic pace of change in multiple domains relevant to decision making and policy formulation in the health sector, again health and non-health domains alike. Additionally, the need to achieve the dual healthcare delivery objectives mentioned earlier calls for healthcare organizations to be increasingly nimble, information transformation and knowledge management, key ingredients for such agility. Many of these hospitals would need to resolve interoperability issues in upgrading their legacy systems that serve these functions currently, or to replace them altogether. In effect, management issues would offer immense opportunities to Canadian software firms to develop and market inventive products and services for payers and management on the one hand and to service the interface between them and the healthcare consumer on the other, for example, the integration of billing systems of payers and providers, and the access points of the consumer. With regard this integration, for example, the ability of the consumer to access billing data by their doctors, and indeed, to access their pricing data, via software, perhaps enterprise system, or web-based, interfaced back-end, with payer systems, offering the latter opportunities for ensuring adequate information presentation to the consumer, who on his/her part is able to confirm services billed. There is no doubt that major software firms would likely be better able to provide the major health information systems of many health jurisdictions, for example, PACS. However, smaller firms also have the opportunity to offer innovative products and services to many of these vertical markets either singly or collaborating with other small and medium-sized software firms, particularly in the area of front-end productivity improvement. This is also a critical issue in the achievement of the dual healthcare delivery goals, and which would command increasing attention in the near future, due to management reorientation towards "private sector" style management, with strict adherence to enhanced productivity, among others. An important point in this regard is the potential lack of interest or outright rejection of these technologies by the very personnel the improvement of whose productivity they aim to achieve. Again and besides the lack of end-use involvement in the project from the start, this negative attitude could also be because of end-user anxiety over possible loss of status, or even job, and technophobia, for examples. Change management programs would resolve many of such issues, and again, underscores the likely market growth in this area. However, software development for front-end and other staff would need to consider the issues, deliberately being non-threatening and user-friendly, as these would be some of the attributes that hospital executives, and health jurisdictions would be seeking in software and other healthcare ICT that they would invest in for productivity-enhancement purposes. Indeed, they would likely be investing quite substantially in the technologies for these purposes, for example customer relations management (CRM) technologies, considering the increasing emphasis on customer-driven healthcare delivery, for example. Thus, several payer and management-related issues would also be key drivers of not just what the health system in Canada would be like in the near future but also the nature and extent of investments in healthcare software and other ICT in the health sector vertical markets in the country. As noted earlier, there would quite significant market openings for software firms regardless of size as recent trends in venture-capital flow into the healthcare-software industry indicate[24]. The Halifax-based software firm, Medusa Medical Technologies, for example, has garnered $4 million in financing lately, evidence that venture capital investors' conviction that healthcare ICT could revolutionize healthcare delivery in the country. In the last, couple of years the firm known for its innovative products and services including to help paramedics collect data and transmit these data wirelessly in real time, facilitating patient treatment , saving lives, and by extension helping to reduce healthcare costs, continues to impress both the healthcare consumer and the capital markets. The firm offers paramedics with a tablet, a notebook-type computer, and touch-screen technology to record every of their action as they treat patients en-route the hospital. According to Scott Campbell, "With the tablet they can record on the fly, as they go…Click, click, in goes a record of administering morphine. Click, click, in goes your adrenaline. Click, click, there's your splint." There is no doubt about the potential of this technology to reduce morbidities and save lives, and it also saves paperwork, enables ER doctors to prepare adequately for treating the patient on arrival, as well as its wealth of data and information being a veritable research pool. The firm need fund injection for its ideas to materialize ideas that likely emanated from the sort of process cycle analyses described earlier, the actualization of which the venture capital mentioned earlier would no doubt kick-start. The firm would receive $2 million in venture capital from private investors in the U.K., and the U.S., with another $1.5 million from Canada. It would also receive $500,000 from Innovacorp, a Crown corporation that invests in early-stage companies in Nova Scotia. The Halifax-based private equity firm Canadian International Capital Inc. is one of the investors, and as Campbell noted, "That gives us the cash to keep our people going until we get to a profitable stage where we can fund the growth from our own business," something that could indeed, happen to other healthcare software start-ups in the country. This underlines the need for them to come up with workable ideas, which would likely emerge from their process analyses and a deeper understanding of the needs of the health sector, or its parts of interests to them. Indeed, other Canadian startups are benefiting from investor largesse, for example, Montreal-based, VisualMed Clinical Solutions Ltd., which in recent years raised $30 million, and $10 million sales-advances for its technologies, termed, "electronic patient records." This electronic system enables accessibility to all lab tests, X-ray reports and other patient data and information physicians using a touch screen to view and update their patients' health records. With the need for hospital and other health institutions, to manage the large quantities of information generated in the health sector becoming clearer to those that mange these establishments, so would the demand for software that would assist in so doing. As Gerard Dab, the chief executive of VisualMed, who is also keen on exploring foreign funding opportunities, particularly in Europe, noted, "All these pieces of information in medicine today are extremely numerous. Today, you've got hundreds of drugs. You've got thousands of tests. How else but through these systems can you handle all this information?" According to Dab, "To get the money we have to get where the money people have an interest in health care, and it's more so in Europe...The financial marketplace still believes that government and private health-care institutions must fix their dysfunction and lack of proper clinical management. Investors believe that hospitals can't be generations behind in computing." These comments though essentially applicable for now, as we noted earlier would not in the near future as even publicly funded health establishments come under increasing pressure to account for the funds allotted to them, and to deliver the goods literally at the same time. The examples of these software firms though suggest that even the smaller ones could raise money for their projects coming up with the right ideas, that is, sound, marketable ideas, whose revenue-generating potential would impress investors and would be difficult for them to ignore. Such ideas would likely emanate from the software firms conducting thorough process cycle analyses on issues such as those we have been discussing, in the health sector, health- and non-health related, but crucial for the eventual outcome of the provision of qualitative and cost-effective health services to Canadians. This also means that the small Canadian firms, which need substantial fund injection to compete effectively in the foreign markets where they often foray, should be keener to explore local markets, which incidentally promise significant openings if only these firms would explore and pursue these opportunities. Medusa, for example bagged a major contract a year and half ago when U.K.-based consultant Accenture Plc collaborated with it to provide systems to 1,500 ambulances in eastern England. Just as the U.K health system is undergoing a major healthcare ICT implementation, connecting hospitals, ambulances, and health centers across the country, creating immense business opportunities for both British software firms and some foreign ones such as Medusa, the Canadian health sector also has many ongoing healthcare ICT projects, and the potential for many more. To be sure, Canadian software firms would also have to compete with foreign software firms eyeing these projects, hence the need for them, in particular having the head-start of being homegrown, to be more aggressive in unearthing even hitherto cryptic business opportunities in the health sector, which process cycle analyses would enable them to do. They should also be prepared to form partnerships with one another in other to facilitate raising capital and to be better able to compete particularly with the larger firms, and perhaps with some foreign firms with plenty of financial resources to spare. Indeed, such partnerships could even be with these foreign firms as some Canadian software are in fact already doing with American vendors. Campbell noted for example that Medtronic Emergency Response System, a major player in the cardiac defibrillation-units market, distributes Medusa' products, noting that his firm needs funds to allow for the development of sales to smaller clients, an indication of the competitive nature of software business, and of the need for Canadian software firms to explore regularly, new market openings.

Exploring the market is a crucial task for Canadian software firms, just as much as marketing their products and services is. They need to know the market in other to develop the products and services that the market needs. As we have observed thus far, knowing the market means appreciating fully the various issues surrounding healthcare delivery in the country. For the purposes of the process cycle analyses that would facilitate such appreciation, these firms would need to decide on those issue they want to explore, based on their strategic objectives, expertise, funding status, and markets of interests among other reasons. As a first step, they should classify these issues into categories also based on their convenience, for examples, into health and non-health issues, or into payer, management, and clinical issues, or system and non-system issues, among other permutations. The whole idea of process cycle analyses is that these issues would need further decomposition, to reveal the sub-issues, and their underlying processes, and again further decomposition and exposition, where the exercise stops based on the firm's goals, and interests, although realizing that opportunities might lurk beneath issues with further decomposition that they would miss with incomplete exploration. A process cycle analysis on any issue should therefore ideally lead to the outcome of healthcare delivery, even if it was just the best way to ensure that practitioners know/remember at the point of care (POC), the size of the needle for use in a spinal tap. The changes that are taking place in medicine, technology, and management bear significance for Canadian software firms. This is even more so in Canada, which appears set for precipitous changes in health funding, with the call for a parallel private health system increasingly louder. Software firms need to be cognizant of these developments, what they mean for market opportunities and the challenges they pose to the firms. These opportunities and challenges would be right across the market spectrum, vertical and horizontal, software firms able to explore both that could offer the products and services these markets need, and that could compete on quality and pricing simultaneously in the markets. It is moot in our discussion here for these reasons to embark on a roll call of the possible products and services that these firms could market to the health sector, as they are legion. What is important is for these firms to know that the opportunities are simply waiting for them to explore. Consider the issue of population aging in Canada. Seniors are some of the most prolific users of the health system, if not the most, and with the population of the elderly in the country likely to increase, should Canadian software firms not be exploring the needs of this population conducting process cycle analyses, and developing the right products and services to meet them? Many of these seniors for example have chronic health problems, affecting multiple organs, for examples, the heart, bones/joints, eyes, and lungs. Many have difficulties moving around due to failing vision, unsteady gait, or memory lapses. Many live too far away from hospitals and clinics hence have restricted access to health services. Many have terminal illnesses, would prefer to receive treatment at home and others do not have people to take them to hospitals even if they wanted to, yet others live in nursing homes. From the viewpoint of the health system, there is not just the need to provide our seniors with qualitative health services, but to do so cost-effectively, which means reducing the hospitalization and prescription medications costs that seniors incur, for examples, without compromising service delivery to them. This means for examples, utilizing ambulatory and domiciliary services more and where appropriate, which in turn means ensuring that these services work. We see right away with the example of seniors that many issues surround health service delivery to this population of Canadians that healthcare software firms could explore and which have immense market potential, that these issues could in fact open up both horizontal and vertical markets, and that not all the market opportunities are self-evident. This example underscores the approach that Canadian software firms should adopt to the health sector that we have stressed in our discussion here. It is of course evident that the health system would need the sort of software for ambulance services mentioned above, that it would need to strengthen its telehealth services, and that it would need to continue to develop its electronic health records (EHR) systems in other to meet the goals of qualitative and cost-effective service provision for seniors. It is also evident tat seniors would need software for examples to help them monitor their health conditions at home, and indeed, with a link to their doctors to alert the latter about changes in the seniors' health that warrant perhaps hospitalization, or some immediate action. However, there is equally no doubt that there are many more possible software and other healthcare ICT that software firms could offer both these markets that they would need to literally dig up during the course of their process cycle analyses. Software firms that engage in these analyses would therefore stand a better chance of availing themselves fully of the immense potential of the health sector, increasing their prospects of profitability. As we previously noted, issues arise even in other sectors of the economy with profound implications for the health sector or that sector might adapt. An example of such developments is the increasing use of advertisement-based business model, companies including software firms, offering products and services free to consumers, raking revenues from advertisements in the process. The recent announcement by Vivendi Universal, the world's biggest music group, that it has reached an agreement to make its music catalogue available on a free legal downloads service exemplifies this trend. Under the agreement, Spiralfrog will offer Universal's songs online in Canada and the United States, a service that New York-based Spiralfrog will launch in December 2006, competing head-on with iTunes services of market leader, Apple, which charges 99 cents per song in the US. This example also illustrates the nature and intensity of the competitive forces in the software industry, which Canadian healthcare software firms should but expect and be ready to confront. In other words, we would likely see this business model emerge in the health sector too, for example, in the area of health information provision, online, with clients offered new and accurate information on different aspects of healthcare and health services delivery of interest to software firms, which would generate revenues from advertisements on these websites[25]. The Vivendi deal aims at the young consumers, and as Spiralfrog CEO Robin Kent noted, "Offering young consumers an easy-to-use alternative to pirated music sites will be compelling." He also noted that his research indicated that in return for free music, youths would not mind the adverts, in particular, so long as the brands and products remain of relevance to them, Spiral frog paying the artists from the advertising revenues. The success of Myspace attest to the workability of advertising-based business models, and with this deal, especially in an industry whose mainstream players, have been particularly opposed to the concept of free downloads, there is likely to be an increasing number of firms embracing the business model, including in the health sector. Software firms could offer these services via a variety of formats, online, as voice or video, or both, in addition to texts, and the materials could actually be downloadable free. In other words, Canadian software interested in the health sector would also need to be flexible as noted earlier to be able to adapt its business models in light of developments within its industry and in the health sector. With, according to the IFPI Digital music report 2006, 60m MP3 players sold globally, 420m single tracks downloaded, music downloads for MP3s, and mobile phones generating revenues of $1.1bn[25], it is no wonder that several firms are offering music downloads. Thus, with HMV and Virgin already offering music downloads, music/TV channel MTV, launching its online store, Urge, and Microsoft gearing up to launch a music store to go with its Toshiba-made, Zune player, which industry pundits assert is a major competitor of the popular, iPod, there must indeed, be market prospects in these endeavors? Should healthcare software firms not therefore be keen to explore these models, to see how they could adapt them to the healthcare sector? Should it not be possible for example to offer healthcare-related products and services in music and video formats that clients could listen to and watch on the go, for example, relaxation and exercise regimes? Could they not in fact present any health promotion, or disease prevention program via a variety of multimedia channels, free, also generating revenues from advertisements? Could this business model not in fact offer smaller healthcare software firms immense business opportunities in the healthcare horizontal markets, without the requirement of significant capital outlays? Much as these prospects sound plausible, would these firms not be better able to capitalize on them if they did their home works, literally, conducting process cycle analyses to discover areas of most needs in the market and developing the appropriate products and services to meet these market needs? There is no gainsaying the need for Canadian healthcare software firms to keep asking questions about what products and services to offer the health sector, for them to thrive in the markets. These questions should in fact cover both the now and the future, as these merge relatively quickly and seamlessly in the health sector. Still on horizontal markets for example, software firms should be keen to know about prospects for individual-owned or payer-based personal health records (PHR) for examples. Canadians would probably like to have more control over their personal health records, as indeed, anyone else would. However, in developing software for this market, which would likely be huge, software firms want to consider the issues involved such as the privacy and confidentiality of the information, particularly if someone else, for example, their doctors and other healthcare professionals, or even health insurers have access to them, the modus operandi for that access, not to mention costs issues. These records could form integral parts of a provincial or even nationwide electronic health records systems with such multi-level access, creating opportunities to develop products and services for the other healthcare stakeholders that record owners could authorize to access the records, for examples, healthcare professionals, or even family members. A recent survey by Healthcare IT News showed that consumers would likely use PHR their health insurers provide, the information in the records available to physicians[26]. In fact, a coalition of healthcare payers in the U.S plans to launch a pilot project that would offer healthcare consumers Web-based PHR in summer 2006, which about 58% of the survey's respondents indicated that they would use. However, 42% said that they would not, concerned among other things by the potential for increased premiums that self-reporting data and information on health habits could engender, underlining the need for software firms to understand all the issues involved in software development projects on which they embark, hence be able to address such concerns. In this instance for example, it might be possible for the skeptical consumers to embrace PHR that would enable them decide the specific information that such health insurers could access. There is no doubt about the need for information sharing in the health sector as this increases the chances of more qualitative service provision, but there is equally the need to filter health information accessible to different cadres of persons and organizations with access to personal health records. Canadian software firms interested in this market would certainly be able to differentiate their value propositions from those of their competitors by paying attention to such details. With more health plans in the U.S for example, ready to reimburse physicians for online healthcare, something that could also happen in Canada with increasing currency, and which access to PHR would no doubt facilitate, the trend toward the convergence of a variety of horizontal and vertical healthcare software and other healthcare ICT seems clear. This would create business opportunities in both markets for software firms, their sizes regardless. Indeed, these opportunities would also be across domain, for example, security technologies not just applied to clinical, administrative, and financial systems, but also to a healthcare organization's wireless and wired milieus. In an atmosphere of limited financial resources, increasing sophistication of consumers' healthcare delivery tastes, pressure to rationalize resource allocation and utilization and to integrate proprietary legacy systems and COTS, the issue of technology convergence would also likely turn out to be a key driver of healthcare software investments in the near future. Canadian software firms would therefore need to focus increasingly on developing "multi-tasking" constitutive software that integrates a variety of the processes that result in a certain outcome, which in combination with others result in the achievement of the dual healthcare delivery objectives mentioned earlier. It would be possible for software firms to discover hence exploit the market opportunities in the health sector. Nonetheless, they should also recognize the importance of their handling of these opportunities in the creation, or otherwise of additional opportunities, as the current issues surrounding the NHS IT program mentioned earlier show. In fact, the British Computer Society (BCS), the chartered institute for IT professionals, hitherto supportive of the IT program, is now supporting the calls for MPs to pursue a technical review of the NHS's £6.2bn computer upgrade, generating serious concerns about the future of the world's largest civilian IT project[27]. The Society wrote a letter of support recently to academics requesting the Commons health committee review, the recent National Audit Office's hardly critical report notwithstanding. Among the concerns by the BCS is a lack of planning in some areas and that a centralized "spine," that BT is building, traversing the country, is probably not a suited match for complex NHS structures. Besides building the "spine," BT is the NHS's lead contractor for delivering new ICT to London, and recently received £1.3m from the NHS for its first two years' work on the £996m, decade-long contract, although it employed between 700 to 1,000 consultants. Experts believe that a change in software partner caused substantial setbacks in the project even as BT says the contract would be profitable. Many ascribe the delays in the project to iSoft, as we noted earlier, whose Lorenzo package for the NHS some even do not think is anywhere near project completion. There is no doubt about inherent software issues creating project delays and budget overruns, but Canadian software firms ought also, as part of the challenges that they face in the health sector, attempt to prevent such problems as much as possible. These problems could no doubt compromise the willingness of investors to commit funds to healthcare software and other ICT, as the case of the BT mentioned above shows. As remote to the direct issues that drive healthcare delivery, and healthcare software investments as some might contend these issues are, project delays and budget overruns, not mention product unreliability, among others, are anathema to the realization of the dual healthcare delivery objectives, hence would unlikely receive top grades, literally, among payers and executives of healthcare organizations. Besides potentially resulting in disfavor for the culprit software firm, such problems could taint the image of the software industry with investors pulling back their funds, a situation in which the industry reeled for many years, and from which it is, in not just the health sector, but also in manufacturing, and other economic sectors just slowly emerging. Clearly, the interplay of drivers, both health and non-health related in determining the direction of healthcare service provision, and by extension of the nature and extent of investments in healthcare software is multidimensional and complex. Yet, a comprehensive understanding of the varieties of interactions between these different drivers would depend on the intent to tease them out methodically, as we have noted in our discussion, for example, via thorough process cycle analyses of the issues and processes of interest. The onus is on Canadian software firms to engage in such painstaking analyses if they were to discover the massive business opportunities that the health sector offers across markets, vertical and horizontal. It is doubtful that any healthcare software firm whose overall strategic objective is to be profitable would ignore an exercise on which its very survival probably depends.

References

1. Available at: http://news.bbc.co.uk/go/pr/fr/-/2/hi/technology/5275544.stm
Accessed on August 23, 2006

2. Young RC. Evidence-based pharmacological treatment of geriatric bipolar disorder. Psychiatr Clin North Am. 2005; 28:837-869, viii.

3. Chambless DL, Ollendick TH. Empirically supported psychological interventions: controversies and evidence. Annu Rev Psychol. 2001; 52:685-716.

4. Available at: http://www.medscape.com/viewarticle/434073_print Accessed on August 23, 2006

5. Available at: http://www.medscape.com/viewarticle/519712 Accessed on August 23, 2006

6. Andersson G, Bergstrom J, Carlbring P, Lindefors N. The use of the Internet in the treatment of anxiety disorders. Curr Opin Psychiatry 2005; 18:73-77.

7. Kenwright M, Marks IM. Computer-aided self-help for phobia/panic via internet at home: a pilot study. Br J Psychiatry 2004; 184:448-449.

8. Colom F, Vieta E, Martinez-Aran A, et al. A randomized trial on the efficacy of group psychoeducation in the prophylaxis of recurrences in bipolar patients whose disease is in remission. Arch Gen Psychiatry. 2003; 60:402-407

9. Colom F, Vieta E, and Sanchez-Moreno J, et al. Stabilizing the stabilizer: group psychoeducation enhances the stability of serum lithium levels. Bipolar Disord. 2005; 7(Suppl 5):32-36.

10. Available at:
http://www.medicalnewstoday.com/healthnews.php?newsid=50120 Accessed on August 24, 2006

11. Available at:
http://www.medicalnewstoday.com/medicalnews.php?newsid=50359
Accessed on August 24, 2006

12. Available at:
http://www.medicalnewstoday.com/medicalnews.php?newsid=50320&nfid=al
Accessed on August 26, 2006

13. Available at: http://www.hc-sc.gc.ca/ahc-asc/media/nr-cp/2006/2006_70_e.html
Accessed on August 22, 2006

14. Available at:
http://www.theglobeandmail.com/servlet/story/RTGAM.20060822.wboca0822/BNStory/specialScienceandHealth/home Accessed on August 24, 2006

15. Available at:
http://news.com.com/Qwest+calls+for+mandatory+data+retention+laws/2100-1028_3-6108279.html Accessed on August 26, 2006

16. Available at:

http://news.com.com/Europe+passes+tough+new+data+retention+laws/2100-7350_3-5995089.html?tag=nl
Accessed on August 26, 2006

17. Available at: http://ca.news.yahoo.com/s/24082006/6/n-usa-qwest-says-calling-data-retention-laws.html
Accessed on August 26, 2006

18. Available at:
http://www.theglobeandmail.com/servlet/story/RTGAM.20060824.whealthcare08243/BNStory/specialScienceandHealth Accessed on August 27, 2006

19. West DM, Miller EA. The digital divide in public e-health: barriers to accessibility and privacy in state health department websites. Journal of Health Care for the Poor and Underserved 17, 652-666, 2006.
Available at:
http://www.medicalnewstoday.com/printerfriendlynews.php?newsid=50539
Accessed on August 27, 2006

20. Available at: http://www.timesonline.co.uk/article/0,,2095-2330116,00.html
Accessed on August 27, 2006

21. Available at:
http://www.bizjournals.com/tampabay/stories/2006/08/21/daily27.html
Accessed on August 27, 2006

22. Available at:
http://www.theglobeandmail.com/servlet/story/RTGAM.20060823.wcma0823/BNStory/specialScienceandHealth Accessed on August 27, 2006

23. Available at:

http://www.medicalnewstoday.com/medicalnews.php?newsid=50346

Accessed on August 27, 2006

24. Available at: http://www.cbc.ca/cp/business/060827/b082710.html

Accessed on August 28, 2006

25. Available at: http://news.bbc.co.uk/go/pr/fr/-/2/hi/business/5294842.stm

Accessed on August 29, 2006

26. Healthcare IT News July 2006, p.6

27. Available at:

http://politics.guardian.co.uk/publicservices/story/0,,1860320,00.html

Accessed on August 29, 2006

Conclusion

The Canadian health sector has entered a new era. From now on, it is no longer a question of whether the sector would invest in healthcare software and other healthcare ICT but rather the extent to which it would. The increasing interest in some quarters, besides, the Supreme Court ruling in 2005 on the subject, on the establishment of a parallel private health system in the country could only highlight the anticipated proclivity of the country's health systems for these technologies in the near future. Indeed, with regard the private health sector, not even the concern of some for the potential for the commoditization of these technologies would likely prevent their widespread adoption in the face of the increasing sophistication of the healthcare services tastes of the Canadian healthcare consumer. In other words, that these technologies could still confer strategic advantage would drive market openings in particular were software firms to embrace some of the ideas we enunciated in this e-book, for example engaging in process cycle analyses to decompose and expose underlying health and non-health issues in their markets of interest.

This exercise as we have so much stressed would reveal opportunities for developing the right product/service mix to meet market needs, also in fact unearth others hitherto unknown or not so evident business opportunities. Again, and as we also have emphasized, the optimization of revenue-generating avenues is bimodal for both the software and health industries, in particular with regard the former, for healthcare organizations in the private sector, although public health systems would also benefit in costs savings if not in direct revenue generation. Thus, both industries would need to undergo continual transformation to enhance the chances of achieving their respective goals. Incidentally, in so doing, for examples, health services in adapting new enterprise-wide supply chain approaches, and software firms, new advertisement-based business models would be creating such opportunities for each other, besides doing so for themselves. Thus, software firms would be able to offer value-added supply-chain management technologies, and the public, and by extension, the health system would benefit from a healthier populace due to free but advertisement-backed health information portals that software firms offer in the above instances. In fact, by broadening the base of subscribers to such health information portals, these firms might even be opening up novel markets for other web-based healthcare products and services for example, personal health records (PHR.)

Canadian software firms therefore have sound reasons to focus a bit more on the country's health sector. Business opportunities would be both vertical and horizontal, and both large and smaller firms would be able to penetrate either market. There is no doubt for example that some projects would be beyond the reach of the smaller software firms due to limitations in financial resources, although, as our discussions, thus far show, venture capital and indeed, other sources of funds could become available to the software firm both from within Canada, and overseas, which has marketable ideas. Again, it is unlikely that those ideas would emerge without a thorough understanding of the issues involved in the firm's markets of interest, which underscores the significance of the process cycle analyses that we have essentially harped on in this e-book. Additionally, the smaller software firms, and even the larger ones would need to be flexible and be ready to modify their business models to capitalize on the many profitable and enduring business openings that would surface in the course of their exploration of market and industry issues.

A s the hospital executive who struggles with synchronizing the maze of data and information before him/her for appropriate decision making would need the software to assist in the process, would the physician keen to access critical patient data and information at the point of care, and the healthcare consumer, to detect changes in its entire physiology. Canadian software firms need to track such needs in different domains, for examples, clinical, administrative, and financial, for trends, both in their needs, and in the technologies evolving to meet them. At the pace knowledge in both Medicine and Technology is changing, we cannot gainsay the need for such tracking, and the applications of new knowledge in the overall strategic orientation exercise that software firms should periodically engage in. The prospects of the software in the health sector would no doubt be tied increasingly to its propensity for due diligence in multiple domains that impinge on its business objectives, in both the short and long terms. Suffice to say that the benefits to such a firm of such market appreciation would undeniably outweigh the costs of the efforts to understand its market of interest, whereas it would incur significant costs, in most probability, to both the software and health industries, and indeed, the country at large, not doing so.

www.ingramcontent.com/pod-product-compliance
Lightning Source LLC
Chambersburg PA
CBHW031238050326
40690CB00007B/861